KING LEAR

SIMPLE SHAKESPEARE SERIES

JEANETTE VIGON

Copyright © 2023 Jeanette Vigon
All rights reserved.
ISBN: 9798323779314

This edition within the "Simple Shakespeare" series is a modern adaptation of William Shakespeare's "King Lear," tailored for a broad audience by simplifying the language and reimagining scenes for contemporary understanding. While it preserves the core story and characters from Shakespeare's original, this version introduces significant modifications aimed at making the timeless tale accessible and engaging for modern readers. The adaptation respects the essence of the original work, offering a bridge between Shakespeare's Elizabethan English and today's vernacular, ensuring that the themes of love, conflict, and fate resonate with a 21st-century audience.

CONTENTS

Why I wrote this book the way I did	ix
Introduction	xiii
ACT I	1
scene 1	3
scene 2	23
scene 3	35
scene 4	39
scene 5	65
ACT II	71
scene 1	73
scene 2	83
scene 3	97
scene 4	99
ACT III	121
scene 1	123
scene 2	127
scene 3	131
scene 4	133
scene 5	147
scene 6	151
scene 7	161
ACT IV	173
scene 1	175
scene 2	183
scene 3	191
scene 4	197
scene 5	201
scene 6	205

scene 7	227
ACT V	235
scene 1	237
scene 2	243
scene 3	245
THE END	275
Further Reading	277
About the Author	281
Afterword	283

WHY I WROTE THIS BOOK THE WAY I DID

Crafting the "Simple Shakespeare" series was an endeavor fueled by a passion to make Shakespeare's timeless tales accessible and relatable to a modern audience, while retaining the essence that has captivated readers for centuries. The decision to reinterpret these classic plays in modern English and in a past tense novel style was rooted in the desire to bridge centuries of linguistic evolution, bringing the stories to life for contemporary readers who may find the original Early Modern English daunting.

The choice of a past tense novel format was a deliberate one, aimed at transforming the dynamic and immediate action of Shakespeare's plays into narratives that unfold with the thoughtful pace and introspection of a novel. This allows readers to immerse themselves deeply in the worlds Shakespeare created, experiencing the depth of character development and plot intricacies in a new light.

Translating Shakespeare's complex language and themes into modern English required careful consideration to preserve the nuanced storytelling and rich emotional tapestry of the original works. It was imperative to maintain the integrity of the stories, ensuring that the modernized versions stay true to the spirit of Shakespeare's intentions. This involved not only translating the language but also adapting the cultural and historical contexts to be more understandable, without diminishing the plays' original meanings and the universal themes they explore.

Furthermore, adapting these plays into a past tense narrative form necessitated a reimagining of Shakespeare's dramatic structure. The original acts and scenes, designed for the stage, were transformed into chapters and sections that flow seamlessly in written form, offering readers a cohesive and engaging narrative journey.

The "Simple Shakespeare" series is an homage to the enduring relevance of Shakespeare's work, crafted with the belief that the core of these stories—themes of love, power, fate, and human nature—are as resonant today as they were in Shakespeare's time. By presenting these tales in a form that is both familiar and fresh, the series aims to spark a new appreciation for Shakespeare among readers who might otherwise shy away from his work due to its original linguistic complexity.

In creating this series, it was my hope to demystify Shakespeare, proving that his plays are not relics of the past but living stories that continue to enlighten, entertain, and inspire. It has been a journey of discovery, not only in translating words but in unveiling the timeless humanity at the heart of Shakespeare's plays. I invite readers to explore these reimagined classics, to find joy in the stories that have shaped our literary heritage, and to see in them reflections of our own lives and times.

It has been a profound privilege to journey through the worlds of Shakespeare in this new light, and I am eager for readers to experience the magic of these stories, told anew.

INTRODUCTION

In this modern English adaptation of "King Lear," William Shakespeare's profound exploration of family, power, and madness is skillfully translated to connect with contemporary audiences while preserving the drama and depth of the original narrative. The setting remains in the royal court of ancient Britain, but the language is updated to reflect today's vernacular, making the tragic story of the aging monarch and his daughters more accessible and relatable.

King Lear, an elderly ruler, decides to divide his kingdom among his three daughters based on who loves him most, setting off a chain of deceit, betrayal, and tragedy. Goneril and Regan, Lear's elder daughters, express false flattery and deceitful intentions to gain their shares of the kingdom, while Cordelia, the youngest and most sincere, faces disinheritance for her stark honesty. This scene strikingly portrays the timeless themes of familial loyalty and the perils of vanity.

As the play progresses, Lear's mental unraveling takes center stage, mirroring the disintegration of order within his kingdom. The Fool accompanies Lear, offering insights wrapped in riddles and humor, highlighting the folly of Lear's decisions and the tragic irony of his situation. This dynamic showcases the complexities of wisdom, folly, and the human condition.

Edmund's subplot as the illegitimate son conniving for legitimacy and power parallels Lear's plot, enriching the themes of betrayal and identity. Edgar, posing as Poor Tom, adds layers of disguise and truth, emphasizing the themes of appearance versus reality.

This adaptation maintains the iconic scenes such as the storm on the heath, where Lear confronts the raw forces of nature and his own frailty, rendered in modern English to enhance the emotional impact and the philosophical depth. The dialogue here captures Lear's existential crisis and his gradual journey towards self-awareness and redemption amidst the chaos of his crumbling world.

By translating Shakespeare's eloquent prose into the modern vernacular, this version makes the narrative accessible while ensuring that the emotional depth and philosophical questions of the original text resonate with today's audience. It invites viewers to experience the tragic beauty of "King Lear," reflecting on the themes of power, justice, family, and redemption that continue to resonate through the ages.

ACT I

SCENE 1

Kent and Gloucester were in King Lear's palace when Kent mentioned he had always thought the king favored the Duke of Albany over the Duke of Cornwall.

"It seemed that way to us," Gloucester agreed. "But now, as the kingdom is divided, it's hard to tell which duke the king prefers. The shares are so evenly balanced, it's impossible to say who is favored."

Kent glanced at the young man standing with Gloucester. "Is this your son?"

. . .

Gloucester nodded, a bit uncomfortable. "Yes, I've raised him. I used to be embarrassed to admit it, but now I'm used to it."

Kent was puzzled. "I'm sorry, I don't follow."

"His mother had him before she was married. Can you believe it?" Gloucester said with a slight chuckle, trying to lighten the mood.

Kent smiled slightly. "Well, the young man turned out quite well regardless."

Gloucester went on, "I have an older son, who is legitimate, but this one, Edmund, was born out of wedlock. Yet his mother was a beauty, and he deserves to be recognized."

Turning to Edmund, he introduced him to Kent. "This is Edmund."

. . .

Edmund bowed politely. "I'm at your service, my lord."

"Remember him as my honorable friend," Gloucester told Kent, putting his hand on Edmund's shoulder.

Edmund responded courteously, "I offer my services to you, Lord Kent."

Kent smiled warmly at Edmund. "I must get to know you better," he said.

"I'll make sure I'm worth your time," Edmund replied earnestly.

Gloucester, looking slightly distracted, mentioned, "He's been away for nine years, and it looks like he'll be leaving again soon. The king is on his way."

Just then, the sound of trumpets announced the arrival of King Lear and his entourage, which included the Dukes of Cornwall and Albany, and his daughters Goneril, Regan, and Cordelia, along with their attendants.

King Lear immediately turned to Gloucester. "See to the lords of France and Burgundy, Gloucester."

"Right away, my liege," Gloucester responded, and he left with Edmund.

Once alone with his family, King Lear declared, "Let's get to the heart of the matter. Bring me the map." He spread the map out before him. "I've decided to divide the kingdom into three parts, to ease the burden of rulership from my old shoulders and pass it on to younger hands. Cornwall, Albany, you both have been like sons to me, and soon you'll receive your portions, just as I will announce the dowries for my daughters to prevent any future disputes. The princes of France and Burgundy have been vying for my youngest daughter's affection, and it's time they received an answer."

. . .

He looked at his daughters. "Now, tell me, which of you loves me the most? I want to reward such love with the greatest share of my kingdom." He gestured to Goneril. "You, my eldest, speak first."

Goneril stepped forward confidently. "Father, I love you more than words can express. More than sight, freedom, and life itself. My love for you is deeper than anything that can be measured or valued."

Off to the side, Cordelia muttered to herself, "What should I do? Just love him and stay quiet?"

King Lear pointed to the expansive lands on the map, from forests to rich plains and broad rivers. "All this, from here to here, I grant to you and your children with Albany, forever," he declared to Goneril.

Turning to his second daughter, he asked, "Now, Regan, my dear, what do you say? You are married to Cornwall. What is your declaration of love?"

. . .

Regan stepped forward, her voice steady. "Father, I am of the same nature as Goneril. Value me as you do her, for in my heart, I express an even greater love. She falls short of my devotion, for I reject all other delights that life can offer, finding my joy solely in your love."

In the background, Cordelia whispered to herself, "Poor me. But perhaps not. I know my love is deeper than my words can show."

Lear then addressed Cordelia, "You, my youngest and no less dear to me, what can you say to gain a share larger than your sisters?"

Cordelia replied simply, "Nothing, my lord."

"Nothing!" Lear exclaimed, taken aback.

"Nothing," she repeated.

. . .

Lear frowned. "Nothing will come of nothing. Speak again."

Cordelia, her tone mixed with sadness, said, "I am sorry, Father, but I cannot speak insincerely. I love you as a daughter should, neither more nor less."

Lear, visibly upset, cautioned her, "Consider your words, Cordelia. They might jeopardize your future."

Cordelia earnestly addressed her father, "Father, you raised me, loved me, and I have always done my duty, obeyed, loved, and honored you in return. If my sisters claim to love you above all else, then why do they have husbands? When I marry, my husband will share my love and duty. I can never promise to love only you, like my sisters do."

King Lear, visibly agitated, questioned her commitment, "Do you truly mean this?"

"Yes, my lord," Cordelia confirmed.

. . .

"So young and so heartless?" Lear challenged.

"So young and so honest, my lord," Cordelia replied softly.

Lear, overcome with disappointment and anger, disowned her dramatically. "Then let your honesty be your dowry. I renounce all my fatherly care and claim to you. From now on, you are as much a stranger to me as the most barbaric Scythian. The man who betrays his own kin could not be more distant from my heart than you, my once daughter."

Kent tried to intervene, "Please, my liege—"

"Silence, Kent! Don't interfere with my anger. I loved Cordelia most, hoping she would care for me in my old age, but no more. Leave my sight!" Lear commanded. "Summon the dukes of France and Burgundy. Let them find her a husband if they can."

He turned to Cornwall and Albany, assigning them the shares of the kingdom and the authority that should have been Cordelia's. "You both will now rule jointly, sharing all the powers and responsibilities of kingship, while I will keep only the title and the rights to be supported by a hundred knights, rotating my residence between your households."

Handing over a part of his crown, he completed the transfer of power. Kent still attempted to reason with him, holding him in high respect, but Lear dismissed him harshly, "The decision is made, stay out of it."

Kent's resolve hardened as he faced Lear's fury. "If speaking truth is uncouth, then let me be rude. What will you do, Lear, when surrounded by yes-men? It is an honor to be honest when authority yields to foolishness. You must reconsider this dreadful decision. Believe me when I say, your youngest daughter loves you deeply; those who speak softly are not always empty of heart."

But Lear was unmoved. "Enough, Kent! Speak no more on pain of death."

. . .

"My life has always been but a tool to protect you," Kent protested, undeterred by the threat. "I fear no loss of it if it ensures your safety."

"Leave my sight!" Lear commanded.

"Please see reason, Lear," Kent pleaded, hoping for a change of heart.

Enraged, Lear invoked the gods, "By Apollo—"

"By Apollo, you swear falsely," Kent interrupted, defiant.

Lear, incensed, reached for his sword. "Traitor!"

Albany and Cornwall intervened, urging, "Please, sir, calm yourself."

Kent continued boldly, "Go ahead, destroy your loyal adviser. But know that if you do not retract your harsh decree, I will keep shouting the truth until I can no longer speak."

Lear issued his final decree, "Listen, traitor! Since you challenge my decisions and disrupt our governance, I grant you five days to prepare for exile. On the sixth, leave my kingdom. If you are found within my lands on the tenth day, you will be executed. This is final."

With that, Kent, once a trusted counselor, was forced to prepare for exile, his loyalty repaid with banishment as Lear's wrath sealed his fate.

Kent, with a resigned yet dignified air, bid farewell to all present. "Farewell, King. Since this is how you choose to be, I find freedom in exile," he declared. Turning to Cordelia, he added, "May the gods protect you, dear girl, for you have thought and spoken justly." Then, addressing Regan and Goneril, he hoped, "May your grand promises be reflected in your actions, and may love truly guide your deeds."

. . .

With these final words, Kent left, ready to start anew in a foreign land.

As Kent exited, Gloucester returned with the King of France, Burgundy, and their attendants. "Here are your suitors, my noble lord," Gloucester announced to Lear.

Lear turned his attention to Burgundy. "We'll speak with you first. You've competed for my daughter's hand. What will you offer for her now, knowing her dowry might be less, or will you end your pursuit?"

Burgundy, maintaining his dignity, responded, "I seek no more than what you have already proposed, and expect no less."

Lear, his tone harsh, replied, "When she was favored by us, we valued her highly, but now her worth has diminished in our eyes. There she stands. If you still want her, despite our displeasure and the small esteem in which we now hold her, she's yours."

. . .

Burgundy hesitated, clearly conflicted. "I am unsure how to respond," he admitted.

Lear pressed him, "Will you take her, with all the disadvantages she now bears—unfriended, hated by us, cursed, and bound by our solemn vow? Decide: take her or leave her."

Burgundy, taken aback by the harsh terms, finally replied, "Forgive me, royal sir, but I cannot commit under these conditions."

King Lear, addressing Burgundy with finality, said, "Then leave her, for I have told you all her worth." Turning to the King of France, his tone softened slightly but still carried a sharp edge, "Great king, I would not mislead you by linking you with someone I disdain. I urge you to set your affections on someone more deserving than this wretch, whom even nature seems ashamed to claim."

The King of France responded, visibly surprised by Lear's harsh words. "It is most strange that she, who was just now the object of your highest praise and the comfort of your old age, should so suddenly be stripped of favor for what appears to be a minor transgression. Her supposed offense must be grave indeed for you to discard such affection, or perhaps it is your affection that has inexplicably soured. I find it hard to believe such a change without a miracle of reason."

Cordelia, in a calm yet firm voice, pleaded with her father, "I ask you, Majesty, to understand that I lack the slickness of speech that speaks without meaning. I act on my intentions without such pretense. Please know that it's not because of any vile act or disgraceful behavior that I've lost your favor, but merely because I lack the art of flattery—which, although costing me your regard, I am glad to be without."

Lear's response was curt and cold. "You would have been better off not born than not to have pleased me as I wished."

The King of France then questioned the very nature of what was unfolding, turning to Burgundy, "Is it merely a slowness to speak what she intends that causes such uproar? What do you say, Burgundy? True love should not hinge on external conditions. She herself is a worthy dowry."

He looked intently at Burgundy, challenging him to reconsider what was truly valuable in Cordelia beyond the material wealth and favor of her father.

Burgundy addressed King Lear with a hopeful tone, "Royal Lear, grant me the dowry you initially proposed, and I will gladly take Cordelia as my wife, making her Duchess of Burgundy."

Lear, unyielding, responded curtly, "Nothing. I have sworn, and I will not waver."

Burgundy, regretful yet resolved, turned to Cordelia, "I am sorry that in losing your father's favor, you also lose a husband."

Cordelia, with quiet dignity, replied, "Peace be with you, Burgundy. Since you value fortune over all, I cannot be your wife."

. . .

The King of France, moved by Cordelia's plight and her steadfastness, then spoke with admiration and resolve, "Fairest Cordelia, you are most precious precisely because you are undervalued by others. Forsaken and yet most worthy, I will cherish the virtues others have discarded. Let it be right that I embrace what has been rejected. It's astonishing how my love has grown where others' care has waned. Your lack of dowry does not diminish your value to me or to France. You will be a queen in our hearts and our land."

He then addressed Lear directly, "You may disown her, but she will be treasured in France. We do not measure her worth by the riches or titles she brings."

Lear, cold and firm, concluded, "She is yours, France. Take her, for I have no daughter like her. I will never see her face again. Go without my blessing."

As Lear left with Burgundy, the King of France urged Cordelia to bid farewell to her sisters.

. . .

Cordelia turned to Goneril and Regan, her eyes clear despite the emotion she felt, "You remain our father's favorites, and I leave you with no ill will. I see your true natures, yet as your sister, I hesitate to voice all I perceive. I entrust our father to your care, hoping you will treat him with the love he expects. If I still held his favor, I would guide him to better care. Farewell, my sisters."

As Cordelia made her dignified departure with the King of France, Regan bristled at her parting advice, "Don't dictate our duties to us."

Goneril dismissed Cordelia sharply, "Focus on pleasing the lord who has accepted you out of pity. You've neglected your duty, and now you're reaping the consequences."

Cordelia responded with a warning, tinged with a hope for justice, "Time will reveal the true nature of deceit; eventually, those who hide their faults are shamed by them. I wish you well."

. . .

With that, Cordelia exited with the King of France, leaving her sisters to their own machinations.

Once alone, Goneril expressed her concerns to Regan, "We need to talk about what concerns us both. I believe our father will leave for your house tonight."

"That's certain, and next month he'll be with us," Regan confirmed, already planning ahead.

Goneril noted the volatility of their father's mood. "You see how changeable he is in his old age. We've both seen it. He always favored Cordelia most, and now he's cast her off without good reason."

"It's his age," Regan observed. "He's never really known himself well."

"The best of his days were impulsive," Goneril added. "Now, we must expect not only his ingrained flaws but also the erratic behavior that comes with old age and illness."

. . .

"We're likely to see more sudden decisions like Kent's banishment," Regan agreed.

"There's still some formality left in his parting from France," Goneril pointed out. "Let's be united in this —if our father continues to wield his power in such an unpredictable manner, his decisions could harm our interests."

"We'll think more on this," Regan decided.

"We must act, and soon," Goneril concluded, signaling the urgency of their situation.

With that, the sisters left to plot their next moves, aware that managing their father's erratic behavior was crucial for maintaining their newly acquired power.

SCENE 2

Edmund stood holding a letter, contemplating the harsh norms of society. "Nature is my only goddess; I follow her rules. Why should I obey society's pointless rules and let them rob me of my rights just because I was born a few years later than my brother? Why call me a bastard? Why deem me lowly? My body is just as strong, my mind as broad, and my form as true as any legitimate child's. Why then am I branded as inferior? Those conceived in secret often possess more vigor and intensity than those born of tedious, passionless unions."

His thoughts darkened as he considered his legitimate brother, Edgar. "I must have your land.

Father loves us both equally, 'legitimate' or not. If this scheme works, I, the so-called lowly one, will rise above the 'legitimate.' I'm on the rise; I will flourish. Now, gods, support us bastards!"

Just then, Gloucester entered, troubled by recent events. "Kent banished, France angrily departed, and the king left tonight, delegating his authority! All these sudden moves! Edmund, what's happening?"

Edmund hid the letter quickly. "Nothing of note, my lord."

"Why were you in such a hurry to put away that letter?" Gloucester asked, curious.

"I have no news, my lord," Edmund replied, trying to sound indifferent.

"What were you reading then?" pressed Gloucester.

. . .

"Nothing, my lord," Edmund said, a mask of innocence on his face.

Gloucester, suspicious, demanded, "No news? Then why the haste to conceal it in your pocket? Nothing has no reason to hide. Let me see it; if it's truly nothing, I won't need glasses."

Edmund pleaded, "Forgive me, sir. It's a letter from my brother, which I haven't fully read. From what I've glanced at, it's not suitable for your eyes."

"Give me the letter," Gloucester insisted.

"I would offend either way, by keeping or giving it. From what I gather, the contents are troubling," Edmund replied.

"Let me read it," Gloucester insisted again.

Edmund hoped for his brother's sake that it was merely an attempt to praise his virtues. Gloucester read aloud, "This reverence for age makes life bitter, withholding our fortunes until we're too old to enjoy them. I'm starting to feel oppressed by elderly tyranny. Come to me, so we can discuss this further. If our father would sleep until I woke him, you could have half his wealth forever, and be favored by your brother, Edgar."

Gloucester's suspicions grew. "Conspiracy! 'Sleep until I woke him, you could have half his wealth.' My son Edgar! Could he have written this? Did he have the wit and heart to concoct such a plan? When did you receive this? Who brought it to you?"

"It wasn't delivered, my lord; that's the cunning of it. I found it tossed into my room through the window," explained Edmund.

"Do you recognize the handwriting as your brother's?" Gloucester inquired.

"If the content were favorable, I'd swear it's his. But considering the nature of it, I hope it's not," replied Edmund cautiously.

. . .

Gloucester accepted the confirmation reluctantly. "It is indeed his handwriting."

"Yes, my lord, it's his handwriting," Edmund affirmed, "but I hope his heart isn't truly in what's written."

"Has he ever suggested such thoughts to you before?" Gloucester questioned, his suspicions deepening.

"Never directly, my lord. However, I've often heard him argue that when sons are fully grown and fathers are aging, the sons should oversee the finances," Edmund explained.

Gloucester was appalled. "The villain! He echoes these very thoughts in the letter! Detestable, unnatural, worse than a brute! Find him—I'll have him arrested. Where is he?"

. . .

"I'm not sure, my lord. If you could hold off your anger until you can get better proof of his intentions, it would be prudent. If you act hastily, you might regret it, harming your own reputation and potentially misjudging his intentions," Edmund cautiously suggested, playing the part of the concerned son.

"Do you really think so?" Gloucester asked, torn.

"If you think it best, I can arrange for you to overhear us discuss this matter tonight. That way, you can be fully assured of the truth," Edmund proposed.

"He can't truly be such a monster," Gloucester hoped aloud.

"He surely isn't," Edmund reassured him.

"To his own father, who loves him so deeply. It's unthinkable!" Gloucester exclaimed, distressed. "Edmund, find him. Guide me to him, use your judgment in setting this up. I would risk everything to know the truth."

. . .

"I will find him immediately, sir, and manage the affair as opportunities arise. I'll keep you informed," Edmund promised, ready to manipulate the situation to his advantage.

Gloucester, deeply troubled, reflected on recent unsettling events. "These recent solar and lunar eclipses do not bode well for us. While some might explain them through natural wisdom, they seem to herald actual misfortunes: love grows cold, friendships falter, brothers grow apart. In cities, there are mutinies; in the countryside, discord; and in palaces, treason. The bond between father and son is strained. This treachery from my own son fits the predictions: son against father. Even the king acts against his nature, father against child. We witness the decline of our era, filled with deceit, emptiness, and betrayal, which follow us relentlessly to our graves. Find this villain, Edmund; it will cost you nothing, and be thorough." With that, he left, disturbed by the disloyalty surrounding him.

Left alone, Edmund scoffed at the human tendency to blame the celestial bodies for their misfortunes.

"It's ludicrous how people, when faced with misfortune—often caused by their own excesses—blame the stars. As if we are villains by necessity, fools by cosmic force, or liars and cheats due to planetary influences! What a clever way for humanity to excuse its vile nature, attributing base desires to the alignment of the stars! My father and mother conceived me under less than ideal astrological signs, suggesting I was destined to be rough and unchaste. Nonsense! I would be exactly who I am regardless of the stars."

As if on cue, Edgar entered, appearing just as Edmund was musing about the cosmic excuse for his schemes. "Perfect timing, Edgar, just like the predictable end of a classic comedy. Here's my chance to play the part of the sorrowful villain, lamenting the tragic divide these eclipses supposedly predict."

Edgar greeted his brother with curiosity. "What's on your mind, Edmund? You seem deeply lost in thought."

. . .

"I was just considering a prophecy I read about recently, regarding the effects of these recent eclipses," Edmund replied, his tone grave.

"Do you really believe in that stuff?" Edgar asked, a bit surprised.

"I assure you, the predictions are dire—strife between children and their parents, death, famine, the breakdown of old friendships, political upheaval, curses upon rulers and nobles, unnecessary mistrust, banishment of friends, loss of allies, failed marriages, and more troubles than I can even list," Edmund elaborated with a hint of manipulation.

"How long have you believed in these astronomical forecasts?" Edgar inquired, half-amused and half-concerned.

"Let's not dwell on that; when did you last see our father?" Edmund changed the subject swiftly.

"Just last night," Edgar replied.

. . .

"Did you talk much?"

"Yes, we spoke for about two hours."

"And how did you part? Was he upset with you in any way?" Edmund probed, searching for any sign of vulnerability.

"Not at all. He seemed perfectly fine," Edgar responded, unaware of Edmund's intentions.

"Think carefully, Edgar. Consider if you might have said something to offend him. I ask you to avoid seeing him for a while. He's quite angry right now—so furious, in fact, that being around you might only make things worse," Edmund lied, setting his trap with a concerned tone.

Edgar, clearly disturbed, expressed his suspicion: "Some villain has wronged me."

. . .

"That's exactly what I'm worried about," Edmund responded with feigned concern. "I urge you to remain patient until our father's anger subsides. Meanwhile, why don't you come and stay at my place? From there, I can arrange for you to meet with him when the time is right. Please, take my key and be cautious. If you must go out, make sure you are armed."

"Armed, brother?" Edgar was taken aback.

"Trust me, it's for the best. Go armed. I wouldn't be honest if I didn't admit there seems to be ill intent directed at you. I've only hinted at the dangers, not fully described the horrors I've heard," Edmund continued, deepening his deceit.

"Will you update me soon?" Edgar asked, hoping for some reassurance.

"Absolutely. I'm here to help you with this," Edmund promised as Edgar, filled with worry, took his leave.

. . .

Once alone, Edmund couldn't help but revel in the ease of his manipulation. "A gullible father and a noble brother, so innocent and honest he suspects nothing. My schemes are smoothly set upon his foolish trust. If I cannot inherit lands by birth, then I'll secure them through my cunning. Everything suits me that I can manipulate to my advantage." With those thoughts, Edmund left to further his plots.

SCENE 3

In the grand hallway of Duke Albany's palace, Goneril, the Duke's wife, confronted Oswald, her steward. A look of annoyance flickered across her face as she asked, "Did my father hit my servant for scolding his jester?"

"Yes, madam," Oswald replied, his voice steady.

Goneril paced, her frustration bubbling over. "Day and night he slights me. Every hour, he erupts into some major misdeed that disrupts us all. I can't tolerate it anymore. His knights are becoming unruly, and he criticizes us for every little thing. When he comes back from his hunt, tell him I'm ill and won't see him. If you're less attentive than before, that's fine. I'll handle any complaints."

Oswald glanced towards the window, then back at Goneril. "He's on his way here now; I can hear him approaching."

Outside, the distant sound of horns filled the air.

Goneril's instructions continued as she walked back toward her chambers. "Act as carelessly as you wish around him and your comrades. I want it to raise questions. If he's upset, he can go complain to my sister, with whom I agree on this matter. That old man still tries to control the powers he's already given away! At this point in his life, he's like a child again and needs to be checked as much as flattered when he steps out of line. Remember what I've told you."

"Understood, madam," Oswald nodded, his expression serious.

. . .

"And make sure his knights are met with cold stares; whatever comes of it doesn't matter. Inform your peers as well. I'm planning to use this situation to speak out. I'll also write to my sister to keep up with our plan. Get ready for dinner."

With a final nod, Oswald turned to leave, and Goneril disappeared into the depths of the palace, her mind racing with plans and anticipation for the confrontations to come.

SCENE 4

Kent, now in disguise, entered the hall with a determined stride. He mused to himself, hoping his new appearance and altered voice would help him execute his plans without recognition. Disgraced and banished, Kent clung to the hope of serving his king incognito and proving his unwavering loyalty.

Just then, the clamor of horns announced King Lear's arrival with his knights and attendants. The king was in no mood to delay, barking orders for dinner as he swept through the hall.

. . .

Spotting Kent, Lear paused, eyeing the unfamiliar face. "Who are you?" he demanded.

"Just a man, sir," Kent replied, his voice steady.

"And what's your business here? What do you want with us?" Lear pressed, scrutinizing Kent.

Kent answered confidently, "I claim to be exactly as I appear. I'm here to serve faithfully anyone who trusts me, to cherish honesty, engage with the wise who speak seldom, to respect justice, to defend myself when necessary, and frankly, I don't care for fish."

Lear, intrigued yet cautious, asked again, "What are you, then?"

"A very honest man, and as poor as the king himself," Kent said with a hint of irony.

. . .

"If you're as poor a subject as he is a king, you're poor enough. What do you seek?" Lear inquired, his interest piqued.

"Employment," Kent stated simply.

"And whom do you wish to serve?"

"You," Kent responded boldly.

"Do you know who I am?" Lear questioned, his gaze narrowing.

"No, sir, but there's something in your presence that makes me want to call you my leader," Kent answered, hoping his respect would mask his familiarity.

Lear raised an eyebrow. "What's that you claim to possess?"

. . .

"Authority," Kent replied, the word carrying a weight of conviction.

"And what services can you offer?" Lear inquired, his interest deepening.

Kent listed his skills with a straightforward air, "I can offer wise counsel, ride, run, spoil a complex story in its telling, and deliver straightforward messages without sugarcoating. I'm skilled in what ordinary men can do, and I pride myself on my diligence."

Lear, assessing Kent's sturdy demeanor, asked, "How old are you?"

Kent responded with a twinkle in his eye, "Not young enough to love a woman just for her singing, nor old enough to dote on her for anything else. I am forty-eight years old."

"Follow me; you shall serve me," Lear decided with a nod. "If I still appreciate your company after dinner, I might just keep you around." He then bellowed for his servants, "Dinner, ho, dinner! Where's my knave? My fool? Someone fetch my fool!"

As one attendant hurried out, Oswald entered the scene briefly, only to be questioned immediately by Lear.

"You there, where's my daughter?" Lear asked sharply.

"Please, your majesty—" Oswald began, but exited before finishing his sentence.

Frustrated, Lear shouted after him, "What did that man say? Bring that idiot back here!" Another knight rushed off in pursuit as Lear continued to call out, "Where's my fool, ho? It seems like the whole world's asleep."

The knight returned shortly, bringing news instead of the fool. "He says, my lord, that your daughter is unwell."

. . .

"Why didn't that servant return when I called him?" King Lear demanded, his voice thick with irritation.

The knight replied cautiously, "Sir, he bluntly said he would not come."

"He would not!" Lear echoed in disbelief.

"My lord, I'm not sure what's happening, but it seems you're not being treated with the same respect and affection as before. There's a noticeable decrease in kindness from everyone, not just the duke and your daughter," the knight explained, his voice laced with concern.

"Is that so?" Lear's voice rose, a mix of anger and surprise.

"I beg your pardon, my lord, if I'm wrong, but I can't keep silent when I see you being wronged," the knight responded earnestly.

. . .

"You're only echoing my own suspicions," Lear admitted, his mood darkening. "I've noticed a subtle neglect recently, which I hoped was just my own paranoia, but perhaps there's more to it. I need to investigate this further. But first, where is my fool? I haven't seen him for two days."

"The fool has been deeply affected since your youngest daughter went to France, sir. He's been very withdrawn," the knight informed him.

"Enough of that; I've taken note," Lear dismissed the concern with a wave of his hand. "Go and tell my daughter I want to speak with her." He watched as an attendant scurried off before turning to another. "And bring me my fool."

As the second attendant left, Oswald re-entered the scene. Lear fixed him with a stern gaze. "You there, come here! Who am I?"

"My lady's father," Oswald replied, his tone cautious.

. . .

"'My lady's father'! You call me 'my lady's father' and not 'king'? You wretch! You mutt! You scoundrel!" Lear erupted, his voice booming with fury.

Oswald, taken aback by Lear's aggression, protested, "I am none of these, my lord; I ask for your forgiveness."

"Do you dare to exchange glares with me, you scoundrel?" Lear snapped, striking Oswald.

"I will not be struck, my lord," Oswald asserted, standing his ground.

Kent, witnessing the disrespect, stepped in, mocking, "Nor tripped either, you lowly soccer player." With a swift move, he tripped Oswald, sending him sprawling.

"I thank you, friend; you serve me well, and you've earned my affection," Lear said, pleased with Kent's loyalty.

. . .

"Get up, sir, let's go! I'll show you what's what," Kent barked at Oswald as he helped him up. "Move along now! If you want to challenge me again, stay, but if not, off you go! Have you no sense?"

With that, Kent shoved Oswald out, clearing the tension for a moment. Lear, appreciating Kent's decisiveness, rewarded him with some money, nodding in approval.

Just then, the Fool entered, breaking the heavy atmosphere. He offered his cap to Kent, jesting, "Let me hire him too: here's my fool's cap."

Lear greeted him warmly, "How are you, my clever lad?"

"Sir, you'd be wise to take my fool's cap," the Fool responded, hinting at the deeper folly in the court's dynamics.

"Why should I take your cap, Fool?" Kent inquired, playing along.

. . .

"Because you're siding with someone out of favor," the Fool explained, his voice tinged with irony. "If you can't adapt to the shifting winds, you'll soon find yourself in trouble. Here, take my cap. This fellow has disowned two of his daughters and turned his back on the third, who actually deserved his blessing. If you follow him, wearing my fool's cap seems fitting."

"How so, uncle? I wish I had two fool's caps and two daughters," the Fool mused aloud.

"And why is that, my boy?" Lear asked, curious despite the jest.

"If I gave everything to them, I'd still keep my fool's caps to myself. Here's mine; go beg another from one of your daughters," the Fool quipped, reflecting the bitter truth behind his humor.

. . .

"Be careful, jester; the whip is near," King Lear warned, his patience wearing thin with the Fool's boldness.

"Truth is a dog that must be sent to the kennel; it must be whipped away, while Lady the hound can linger by the fire and stink," the Fool retorted, unphased by the threat.

Lear shook his head, annoyed. "You're nothing but a headache to me!"

"Sir, let me teach you a piece of wisdom," the Fool offered, ignoring Lear's irritation.

"Go on, then," Lear grumbled, resigned.

The Fool recited his advice with a playful tone:
    "Show less than you have,
    Speak less than you know,
    Lend less than you owe,
    Travel more than you plan,
    Learn more than you assume,
    Gamble less than you can;

Abandon your drink and your dalliances,
Stay indoors,
And you'll end up with far more
Than mere forty in store."

Kent, listening to the rhyme, dismissed it, "This is nonsense, Fool."

"Then it's like the breath of a lawyer who's not been paid; you gave me nothing for it. Can't you see the value in nothing, uncle?" the Fool quipped back.

"Why, no, boy; you can't make something out of nothing," Lear responded, echoing a familiar lesson.

The Fool turned to Kent and suggested, "[To Kent] Please, tell him how much his land was worth; he won't listen to a fool."

"A sharp-tongued fool!" Lear remarked, half in exasperation, half in amusement.

. . .

"Do you know the difference, my boy, between a sour fool and a sweet one?" the Fool asked, drawing Lear's attention.

"No, lad; enlighten me," Lear encouraged, intrigued despite himself.

The Fool laid out his riddle with a sly grin:
"The lord who advised you
To part with your land,
Let him stand by me,
And you take his place:
The sweet and sour fools
Will soon show their faces;
The jester wears his motley here,
The other's folly is found out there."

"Do you call me a fool, boy?" King Lear demanded, his tone sharpening.

"You've given away all your other titles; that's the one you were born with," the Fool shot back with fearless candor.

. . .

Kent, watching the exchange, remarked, "He's not just a fool, my lord."

"No, indeed," the Fool agreed, "lords and great men won't allow it; if I had a monopoly on foolishness, they'd demand a share, and so would the ladies. They can't let me be the only fool; they're always reaching for a piece." He then playfully proposed, "Give me an egg, uncle, and I'll give you two crowns."

"And what two crowns would those be?" Lear asked, playing along despite his growing frustration.

The Fool explained with a mischievous grin, "When I split the egg down the middle and eat the contents, you'll have the two halves of the shell—just like when you divided your kingdom and gave it all away, you ended up carrying the burden on your own back. You had little sense on your bare head when you gave your golden crown away. If I'm speaking truthfully, let the one who disagrees be whipped."

He then burst into song:
 "Fools had never less sense in a year;

For wise men have turned foolish,
They don't know how to use their brains,
Their behavior is so childish."

"When did you start being so fond of songs?" Lear asked, his curiosity piqued despite the Fool's sharp words.

"I've been singing ever since you turned your daughters into your mothers. When you handed them the authority and stripped yourself of dignity," the Fool sang again:
"Then they cried with sudden joy,
And I sang from sorrow,
That a king should stoop so low,
And join the fools, however."

"Please, uncle, hire a schoolmaster to teach your fool how to lie; I really want to learn," the Fool continued, half-joking, half-serious.

"If you lie, boy, we'll have you whipped," Lear responded, not entirely sure how to handle his provocative yet insightful jester.

. . .

The Fool, always ready with a sharp observation, lamented the precarious position his honesty put him in. "I wonder about the family ties between you and your daughters. They would have me whipped for telling the truth, you would have me whipped for lying, and sometimes I'm even whipped for saying nothing at all. I'd rather be anything than a fool, and yet, I wouldn't want to be you, uncle. You've shaved away your wit from both sides, leaving nothing in the middle. Ah, here comes one of those shavings now."

As Goneril entered, King Lear turned to her, noting her stern expression. "What's with that scowl, daughter? You seem to frown too much these days."

The Fool, seizing the moment, quipped, "You were quite the man when you didn't care about her frowns. Now, you're just a zero without any value. I'm better off; I'm a fool, you are nothing." Turning to Goneril, he continued, "Yes, indeed, I'll hold my tongue because your face commands it, though you say nothing. Quiet, quiet. He who keeps neither bread nor bits will soon be in want." He then gestured towards Lear, "There goes an empty husk of a man."

Goneril addressed her father with a tone of frustration and concern. "Not only this fool, but others in your bold entourage constantly stir up trouble and quarrel incessantly, causing unbearable disturbances. I thought to bring this to your attention in hopes of finding a remedy. But now, seeing your recent actions and words, I fear you might be encouraging this behavior. If so, such conduct cannot escape criticism, nor will the necessary corrections be overlooked, which, in the pursuit of a healthy state, could harm you in ways that would be shameful if not addressed as required."

The Fool interjected a pointed analogy to emphasize Goneril's point, "You know, uncle, the hedge-sparrow fed the cuckoo until the cuckoo turned on it and bit off its head. Just like that, the light went out, and we were left in the dark." His words hung in the air, a stark warning cloaked in the guise of simplicity.

. . .

Lear, visibly shaken and bewildered by the confrontation, questioned his relationship with Goneril, "Are you truly my daughter?"

Goneril responded, urging moderation, "Please, sir, I wish you would use the good judgment I know you possess, and set aside these recent changes that have so altered you from your true self."

The Fool, ever ready with a jibe, interjected, "Can't an ass know when the cart is pulling the horse? Whoop, Jug! I love thee."

Lear, his voice laden with confusion and despair, appealed to those around him, "Does anyone here recognize me? This isn't Lear. Does Lear walk like this, talk like this? Where are his eyes? Perhaps my perception is weakening, or my discernment is clouded— Am I awake? This can't be right." He paused, then desperately asked, "Who can tell me who I am?"

"Lear's shadow," the Fool replied succinctly, highlighting Lear's loss of self and substance.

. . .

"I wish to understand that," Lear murmured, wrestling with his identity. "By all traditional signs of power and wisdom, I am led to believe I no longer have daughters."

The Fool cryptically noted, "Which they will turn you into an obedient father."

Lear, seeking some clarity amidst the chaos, asked Goneril, "Your name, fair gentlewoman?"

Goneril, frustrated with her father's demeanor, tried to steer the conversation back to practical issues, "This wonderment, sir, is akin to your other recent antics. I urge you to see my intentions correctly: you are old and should be wise. Here, you maintain a retinue of a hundred knights and squires, whose unruly and wild behavior has turned our court into a den of debauchery, resembling a tavern or brothel more than a noble palace. The disgrace calls for immediate action. I implore you, as your daughter, to reduce your entourage. Those who remain should befit your age and station, and conduct themselves respectfully."

. . .

Infuriated by her words and his own growing paranoia, Lear exploded, "Darkness and devils! Saddle my horses; gather my men: You degenerate bastard! I will not bother you further." His mind reeled, grappling with the remnants of his authority and the betrayal he felt, "Yet I still have another daughter."

Goneril stood her ground as Lear's wrath grew, asserting, "You strike my people; and your disorderly followers treat their superiors as servants."

At that moment, Albany entered the scene. Lear, his emotions raw and bubbling over, cried out in anguish, "Woe to me, for repenting too late—" Turning to Albany, he pleaded desperately, "Oh, are you here, sir? Is this your doing? Speak, sir. Prepare my horses." His voice hardened as he spoke of betrayal, "Ingratitude, you marble-hearted fiend, more hideous when it shows itself in a child than any sea monster!"

"Please, sir, be patient," Albany implored, trying to calm the escalating tension.

. . .

Lear, addressing Goneril with scorn, accused, "Detestable vulture! You lie. My followers are men of choice and rarest qualities, who fully know their duties and uphold the honor of their names with utmost precision." His thoughts then turned bitterly to his youngest daughter, Cordelia, "Oh, such a minor fault, yet how monstrous it appeared in Cordelia, wrenching my very nature from its place, draining all love from my heart, adding only bitterness. Oh, Lear, Lear, Lear!" He lamented, striking his head, "This head opened to folly and forced out wise judgment. Leave, leave, all of you."

Albany, caught off guard by Lear's furious outburst, responded, "My lord, I assure you, I am as innocent as I am unaware of what has provoked you."

"It may be so," Lear conceded, his voice carrying a mix of despair and resignation. He then raised his voice to the heavens, "Hear me, nature, hear; dear goddess, hear! If you intended to make this woman fruitful, I pray you make her barren! Dry up the very source of her fertility, and if she must bear a child, let it be a bitter creature that brings her torment and disgrace! May it age her with worry and constant tears, and turn all her maternal joys to disdain, so she may know how painful it is to have a thankless child!" With that curse, he stormed off.

Albany, left in the wake of Lear's tempest, looked upwards, bewildered and distressed, murmuring to the heavens, "Now, gods that we worship, where does this all stem from?"

Reentering in a storm of emotion, King Lear exclaimed, "What, fifty of my followers dismissed at once! Within a fortnight!"

Albany, concerned and confused, asked, "What's the matter, sir?"

Lear turned fiercely to Goneril, his voice laden with pain and anger, "Life and death! I am ashamed that you have the power to so deeply affect my manhood; that these involuntary tears should honor you! May curses and mists fall upon you! The wounds a father's curse inflicts may they pierce your every sense! If these old, foolish eyes weep for this again, I'll tear them out and use their tears to soften clay. Has it truly come to this? So be it: yet I still have another daughter, whom I am certain is kind and caring. When she learns of your actions, she'll scratch your wolfish face with her nails. You will see—I will reclaim the dignity you think I have shed forever."

With that, Lear stormed off with Kent and his attendants, leaving a tense silence behind.

Goneril turned to Albany, seeking affirmation, "Did you see that, my lord?"

Albany, struggling to reconcile his loyalty to his wife with the scene he had just witnessed, replied, "I cannot be so biased, Goneril, despite my love for you—"

"Enough," Goneril cut him off sharply. "Oswald! And you," she turned to the Fool, disdainfully, "you're more knave than fool, following your master."

The Fool, catching the mood of departure and echoing Lear's sentiments with a rhyme, called out,

"Uncle Lear, Uncle Lear, wait and take the fool with you. A fox, once caught, and such a daughter, should surely be led to slaughter. If my cap could buy a rope, then the fool would follow in hope."

With a dramatic flair, the Fool then exited, leaving Goneril to reflect on the strategic wisdom of allowing Lear his knights. She mused aloud, "This man has received good counsel—keeping a hundred knights is both politic and safe. With them at his command, he can chase every whim, each irritation and fantasy, defending his frailty with their strength, and hold our lives at his mercy. Oswald, come here!" Her words hung heavily, a blend of strategy and unease about the power Lear retained.

Albany cautiously advised, "Well, you may fear too far."

Goneril retorted with firm conviction, "It's safer than trusting too far. Let me prevent the dangers I fear rather than live in fear of them: I know his heart. I've already written to my sister about what he's said; if she agrees to sustain him and his hundred knights after I've pointed out the unfitness—"

. . .

Their conversation was interrupted by the return of Oswald. Goneril quickly addressed him, "How now, Oswald! Have you written that letter to my sister?"

"Yes, madam," Oswald replied promptly.

"Take some company, and hurry to horse," Goneril instructed, eager to reinforce her position. "Inform her fully of my particular concerns, and add any arguments you think will make the case stronger. Go now, and hurry back."

As Oswald departed to carry out her orders, Goneril turned back to Albany, who was clearly uneasy with her aggressive approach. "No, no, my lord, this gentle manner of yours, though I don't condemn it, may I say without offense, shows more lack of wisdom than it does praiseworthy gentleness."

Albany, trying to offer a different perspective, responded, "How far your eyes may see, I cannot tell.

But sometimes, in our attempt to improve, we ruin what was already good."

"Nay, then—," Goneril began to argue, but Albany cut her off, concluding the discussion with, "Well, well; let's see what happens."

With that, they exited, leaving the future of their actions uncertain and the consequences yet to unfold.

SCENE 5

ing Lear, along with Kent and the Fool, stood in the court before Gloucester's castle. Lear handed a set of letters to Kent.

"Take these to Gloucester," Lear instructed. "Tell my daughter only what she asks for from the letter. Be quick about it, or I'll get there before you."

Kent nodded earnestly. "I won't rest, my lord, until your letter is safely delivered."

. . .

As Kent hurried off, the Fool quipped, "If a man's brains were in his heels, wouldn't they be in danger of getting frostbite?"

"Yes, boy," Lear responded, amused.

"Then cheer up! Your sharp mind should never drag," the Fool smiled.

Lear laughed heartily.

"You'll see, your other daughter will treat you well," the Fool continued, his tone playful yet edged with a hint of seriousness. "Even though she resembles her sister as much as a crab resembles an apple, I know what I know."

"And what do you know, my boy?" Lear asked, curiosity piqued.

. . .

"She will be as much like her sister as one crab is to another. Can you guess why a nose is in the middle of a face?"

"No," Lear admitted.

"To keep the eyes from being too close, so what you can't smell, you might see," the Fool explained, then his tone softened. "I think you were unfair to her—"

"Can you tell how an oyster makes its shell?" Lear cut in, shifting the subject.

"No," the Fool shook his head, "but I can tell you why a snail has a shell."

"Why's that?"

"To keep his head safe," the Fool said pointedly. "Not to give it away to his daughters, leaving himself unprotected."

. . .

Lear, struggling with his emotions, declared, "I must forget my own feelings. So much for being a kind father! Are my horses ready?"

"Your servants are seeing to them," the Fool responded, then added with a playful twist, "The reason why there are only seven stars is quite a simple one."

"Because there aren't eight?" Lear guessed, playing along.

"Exactly, you'd do well as a fool yourself," the Fool chuckled.

Lear, feeling the sting of betrayal, lamented, "To think I must take it all back by force! Such monstrous ingratitude!"

"If you were my fool, uncle, I'd scold you for growing old before becoming wise," the Fool teased.

. . .

"How do you mean?" Lear asked, puzzled.

"You shouldn't have grown old before you grew wise," the Fool pointed out.

Lear, his voice tinged with despair, pleaded, "Oh, let me not go mad, sweet heaven, keep me sane. I do not wish to lose my mind!"

At that moment, a gentleman entered. "Are the horses ready?" Lear asked him urgently.

"They are, my lord," the gentleman confirmed.

"Come, boy," Lear beckoned to the Fool.

As they prepared to leave, the Fool couldn't resist one last jest, "The girl who laughs now as I leave will soon no longer be a maid, unless fate cuts her laughter short."

. . .

With that, they all departed.

ACT II

SCENE 1

Edmund greeted Curan as he entered. "Hello, Curan."

Curan responded, "Hello to you too, sir. I've just come from your father's place. I told him the Duke of Cornwall and his wife, Regan, will arrive here tonight."

Edmund, puzzled, asked, "Why are they coming?"

. . .

"I'm not sure," Curan admitted. "Have you heard the latest rumors? The quiet ones that people only whisper about?"

Edmund shook his head. "No, what are they?"

Curan leaned in closer, lowering his voice. "There's talk of possible wars brewing between the Dukes of Cornwall and Albany. Have you heard anything about that?"

"Not a word," said Edmund.

"You might hear something soon. Take care, Edmund." With that, Curan left.

Alone, Edmund pondered the news. "The duke is coming tonight? Perfect! This will fit into my plans perfectly." He knew his father had ordered guards to capture his brother, and Edmund had his own plans that needed quick action. "I need to act fast and hope for a bit of luck."

. . .

He called out to his brother Edgar, who was hiding. "Edgar, come down here!"

Edgar appeared, cautious and wary.

"Our father has set guards on you. Someone knows where you're hiding. You have the cover of night to escape. Have you said anything against the Duke of Cornwall? He's on his way here, and so is Regan. Think carefully if you've spoken against their ally, the Duke of Albany. You need to be careful."

Edgar assured him, "I swear, I haven't said a word."

Suddenly, Edmund tensed. "I hear our father coming. Forgive me for what I must do next.' He drew his sword. "Defend yourself, just for show. Now, act convincingly. Yield, and follow my lead. Quick, before our father! Run, brother, run! Get some torches over here! Farewell!" Edgar escaped into the darkness.

. . .

Alone, Edmund needed to make his deception believable. He cut his own arm lightly. "This should look like I've struggled fiercely," he muttered, recalling how he'd seen drunkards fake worse injuries for fun. "Father, father! Help, help!"

Gloucester rushed in with servants, their torches flickering in the dark. "Edmund, where's the villain?"

"He was right here, sword drawn, muttering dark spells and trying to conjure the moon," Edmund lied, playing into his father's fears.

"But where is he now?" Gloucester pressed, looking around anxiously.

"I'm bleeding, look at me," Edmund pointed to his wound to distract his father.

"Where did he go, Edmund?" Gloucester insisted.

. . .

"He ran this way when he realized he couldn't convince me to kill you," Edmund continued his tale. "I warned him about the gods' wrath against those who harm their parents. I told him about the strong bond between father and child. Seeing how strongly I opposed his wicked plan, he attacked me unexpectedly, wounding my arm. But when he saw my resolve, or perhaps scared by the noise, he fled suddenly."

"Let him escape far from here," Gloucester declared with fury. "He shall not remain free in this land. If found, he must be dealt with swiftly. The noble duke, my lord and patron who arrives tonight, will affirm this. By his authority, I will declare that anyone who captures him will earn our gratitude by bringing this murderous coward to justice. Anyone hiding him will face death."

Edmund continued to weave his deceitful narrative. "When I tried to talk him out of his plans and realized he was determined to proceed, I threatened to expose him. Furious, he scoffed at me, calling me a worthless bastard. He argued that no one would trust my word over his, claiming that even if I showed proof like his own letter, he would deny it and accuse me of scheming against him. He believed everyone would assume I wanted him dead for my own gain."

Gloucester shook his head, disgusted. "A stubborn and entrenched villain! Would he really deny his own written words? I cannot fathom it." Just then, trumpets sounded in the distance, signaling the duke's arrival. "I don't know why he's here now. I will secure all ports; the villain won't escape. The duke will surely support this. Moreover, I will distribute his portrait far and wide so the entire kingdom recognizes him. As for you, my loyal and true son, I will ensure you have the means to inherit my lands."

Just then, Cornwall, Regan, and their attendants arrived. Cornwall greeted Gloucester warmly, "How are you, my noble friend? I've just arrived and already I've heard troubling news."

"If these rumors are true, no punishment seems harsh enough for such a criminal," Regan added, showing concern for Gloucester.

. . .

"Oh, madam," Gloucester replied, his voice laden with sorrow, "my old heart is broken, truly broken!"

"Did my father's godson, the one he treated like his own son—your Edgar—try to take your life?" Regan asked incredulously.

Gloucester, ashamed and distressed, replied, "Oh, lady, it's a disgraceful matter that ought to be kept secret."

Regan pressed further, "Wasn't Edgar associating with those rowdy knights who follow my father?"

"I'm not sure, madam; it's all very troubling," Gloucester responded, his voice filled with uncertainty.

Edmund, seizing the opportunity, confirmed, "Yes, madam, he was indeed part of that group."

. . .

Regan nodded, her suspicion growing. "It's no wonder then that he turned out so badly. Those knights are known for their bad influence. They must have encouraged Edgar to plot for the old man's demise to squander his wealth. Just tonight, my sister gave me a thorough warning about them. She advised that if they plan to stay at my house, I should stay away."

Cornwall agreed, "I won't be there either, Regan. Edmund, I hear you've been quite the dutiful son to your father."

"It was my obligation, sir," Edmund replied humbly.

Gloucester added, "He exposed Edgar's scheme and was injured while trying to stop him."

Cornwall was concerned. "Is Edgar being pursued?"

"Yes, my lord," Gloucester confirmed.

. . .

"If he's caught, he won't be a threat anymore," Cornwall declared. "Use my resources as you see fit. Edmund, your loyalty and obedience have greatly impressed us today. We need people we can trust deeply, and you have proven yourself. You will join us."

"I am at your service, sir, fully and faithfully," Edmund responded with a hint of triumph.

Gloucester expressed his gratitude, "Thank you, your grace."

Cornwall then shared, "You might wonder why we've come so unexpectedly, traveling through the night. There are important matters at hand that require your wise counsel, Gloucester. Both our father and sister have written to us about some issues. We thought it best not to handle them from afar. The messengers are waiting for our response."

Gloucester assured them, "I am at your service, madam. You and your graces are most welcome here."

. . .

With plans to discuss further, they all exited, leaving the castle hall filled with the weight of unfolding schemes and family discord.

SCENE 2

As the dawn broke, Kent and Oswald entered the grounds of Gloucester's castle from opposite sides. They met unexpectedly.

"Good morning to you, friend. Do you belong to this house?" Oswald asked, his tone polite yet cautious.

"Yes," Kent replied succinctly.

"Where can we stable our horses?" Oswald inquired, looking around for a suitable spot.

. . .

"In the mud," Kent responded dryly, a slight smirk on his face.

"Please, if you care about me at all, give me a straight answer," Oswald pressed, his frustration beginning to show.

"I don't care about you," Kent said bluntly.

"Well, then, I suppose your opinion doesn't matter to me," Oswald retorted, trying to mask his irritation.

"If I had you confined in a small pen, you'd start to care," Kent threatened lightly, his eyes gleaming with a challenge.

"Why are you treating me this way? I don't even know you," Oswald protested, his confusion turning into anger.

"But I know you," Kent countered, stepping closer.

. . .

"And what exactly do you think you know about me?" Oswald demanded, his pride wounded.

"You're a knave and a scoundrel, scavenging leftovers, lowly and arrogant. A man of cheap fabric and cheaper virtue. You're cowardly, a flatterer, excessively precise and utterly servile," Kent listed scornfully. "A man who'd sell honor for service, nothing more than a mix of a rogue, a beggar, a coward, and far worse, the offspring of deceit: someone I'd gladly punish if you deny any part of this truth."

Oswald stepped back, astonished and enraged by the harshness of Kent's words. "What kind of monster are you, to attack someone who neither wrongs you nor even knows you?" he exclaimed, his voice echoing in the early morning air.

Kent's anger flared up as he faced Oswald. "How shameless can you be to deny knowing me? Wasn't it just two days ago that I tripped you and beat you in front of the king? Draw your sword, you scoundrel! Though it's night, the moon is out. I swear I'll thrash you under this moonlight. Draw, you worthless scamp!" he exclaimed, unsheathing his sword.

"Stay away! I want nothing to do with you," Oswald replied, stepping back, his voice trembling.

"Draw your sword! You come bearing letters against the king and dare to undermine his authority. Draw, or I swear I'll slice you up!" Kent threatened, moving aggressively towards Oswald.

"Help! Someone help me! Murder!" Oswald cried out, desperation in his voice as Kent began to strike him.

Just then, Edmund rushed in with his sword drawn, followed closely by Cornwall, Regan, Gloucester, and several servants.

"What is happening here?" Edmund demanded, looking around at the commotion.

. . .

Kent, still in a fury, turned to Edmund. "Care to join the fight, young sir? Come, I'll give you a taste of battle!"

Gloucester, alarmed, called out, "Weapons down! What is going on here?"

Cornwall stepped forward, his voice authoritative. "Everyone, keep calm! The next person to strike will pay with his life. Now, what's the problem here?"

Regan pointed out, "These are the messengers from our sister and the king."

Cornwall looked between them. "What's the disagreement? Speak up!"

Oswald, catching his breath and visibly shaken, managed to say, "My lord, I'm barely able to speak."

Kent's voice was tinged with mockery as he addressed Oswald. "No wonder you're so out of breath, having mustered up what little courage you have. You spineless fool, even nature rejects you—a tailor must have stitched you together!"

Cornwall, puzzled by Kent's words, interjected, "A strange claim, that a tailor can make a man?"

"Yes, a tailor," Kent retorted sharply. "Even a stonecutter or a painter couldn't have crafted him so poorly, even if they had only been at their trade for two hours."

Cornwall, trying to understand the root of the conflict, asked, "How did this quarrel start?"

"This old brute," Oswald began, gesturing towards Kent, "whose life I spared only because of his age—"

Kent cut him off furiously, "You miserable creature, you unnecessary thing! My lord, allow me to crush this crumb of a man into paste and plaster it on the walls of the privy. Spare you for my grey beard? Don't make me laugh, you whelp!"

. . .

"Calm yourself!" Cornwall commanded, glaring at Kent. "You disgraceful man, don't you have any respect?"

"Yes, sir, but my anger is justified," Kent shot back.

"Why are you so angry?" Cornwall pressed.

"That someone as deceitful as this man can carry a sword, when he possesses no shred of honesty," Kent exclaimed. "Men like him, with their deceitful smiles, are capable of severing the sacred bonds too entangled to untie. They fan the flames of discord and cool the warmth of friendship as it suits them, changing their loyalties as quickly as the wind shifts, knowing nothing but to follow their masters like dogs. A curse on your mocking face! Do you think I'm a fool to be laughed at? If I had you on the plains of Salisbury, I'd chase you back to Camelot myself!"

"Why, are you out of your mind, old man?" Cornwall asked, taken aback by Kent's ferocity.

. . .

Gloucester, hoping to resolve the matter, inquired, "What caused the disagreement? Tell us."

"There's no greater animosity than what exists between me and this scoundrel," Kent declared, his disdain for Oswald palpable.

Cornwall's frustration was evident as he questioned Kent's animosity. "Why do you call him a knave? What has he done?"

Kent's response was terse. "I simply don't like his looks."

"That could be said about anyone's face here, including mine, his, or hers," Cornwall replied, gesturing to the faces around them.

"Sir, I am known for my honesty," Kent explained. "I've seen better faces than any present here today."

. . .

Cornwall assessed Kent, his tone tinged with skepticism. "You seem to be one of those men who, praised once for being direct, now overplay their roughness, straying far from their true nature. You claim honesty and plain speaking, and perhaps you think that's a virtue. I know this type: their so-called plainness often hides deeper schemes and corruption than those who openly curry favor."

"Truly, sir," Kent began with a respectful tone, "under your imposing presence, which shines as brightly as the sun, I must clarify—I am no flatterer. If someone deceived you with straightforward talk, he was just a simple knave. And I refuse to be such, even if it means losing your favor."

Cornwall, growing impatient with the philosophical discussion, pressed further. "What exactly did you do to offend him?"

Oswald finally spoke up, his voice carrying a mix of defensiveness and exhaustion. "I did nothing to him personally. It was only recently that the king, misinterpreting something, decided to strike me. When he did, Kent saw an opportunity to curry favor with the king by tripping me and attacking me while I was down. He insulted me vehemently and made a spectacle of the situation, which somehow earned him praise from the king. He took advantage of my vulnerable state to boost his own standing, and now he has targeted me again here."

As the argument escalated, Cornwall ordered sternly, "Bring out the stocks! You stubborn old fool, you self-important relic, we'll teach you a lesson."

Kent stood his ground, unyielding. "Sir, I am too old to be schooled like a child. Do not call for your stocks for me. I am here on the king's business. By treating me this way, you show little respect and reveal your hostility towards the king himself by punishing his envoy."

But Cornwall was resolute, "Bring forth the stocks! As long as I live and hold my honor, he will sit there until noon."

Regan, with a cruel twist of her lips, added, "Until noon! Till night, my lord, and all night too."

. . .

Kent, shocked by her harshness, replied, "Madam, if I were as lowly as your father's dog, you wouldn't treat me so harshly."

"Sir, since you are his servant, I will," Regan retorted coldly.

Cornwall, nodding in agreement, declared, "This man is just like the one our sister warned us about. Bring the stocks here!"

As the stocks were brought out, Gloucester made a final plea to Cornwall, "Your grace, please reconsider this. His offense may be great, but his king will reprimand him. The punishment you are about to inflict is usually reserved for the lowest criminals, for petty thieves and common trespassers. The king will surely be displeased to see his messenger treated so trivially."

Cornwall dismissed Gloucester's concerns briskly, "I'll take responsibility for that."

. . .

As Kent's legs were locked into the stocks, Regan coldly oversaw the punishment. "My sister would take it far worse if her servant were mistreated for simply carrying out her orders. Put his legs in," she commanded, ensuring Kent was immobilized.

With Kent secured, Regan turned to Cornwall. "Let's leave this place," she said, and they exited, leaving only Gloucester and Kent behind.

Gloucester expressed his sympathy, "I'm sorry to see this happen to you, friend. It's the duke's will, and as you know, his mind cannot be changed easily. I'll try to speak on your behalf."

"Please, don't trouble yourself," Kent responded wearily. "I've been on the road for a long time and hardly slept. I might as well rest here. Eventually, fortune may turn again. Good morning to you."

As Gloucester departed, lamenting the injustice, Kent turned his thoughts to higher matters. "Good king," he murmured, looking skyward, "you are like a blessing from heaven warming me like the sun."

Kent then focused on a letter he had on him, holding it up to catch the moon's faint glow. "This must be from Cordelia," he guessed, knowing she had somehow learned of his troubles. "She has always been my beacon, guiding me through darkness. In these difficult times, she seeks to heal the wounds inflicted by fate."

Exhausted and overwhelmed, Kent decided not to dwell on his grim situation. "Let fortune turn once more," he sighed, settling into an uneasy sleep in the uncomfortable stocks, hoping for a reprieve from his misfortunes.

SCENE 3

Edgar entered the wooded area, a place he hoped would offer him shelter and a chance to think. He had narrowly escaped capture, hiding in the hollow of a tree while those pursuing him passed by. "No place is safe," he muttered to himself, "everywhere I go, someone is there, waiting to catch me."

Determined to remain free as long as possible, Edgar decided to disguise himself in the most humble and ragged appearance imaginable. "I'll smear dirt on my face, wear a simple blanket around my waist, and tangle my hair as if I've been touched by elves," he planned, imagining how he would brave the elements in his new guise. This, he thought, would shield him from the harsh scrutiny of the world.

He recalled seeing beggars from Bedlam, their voices loud and haunting as they struck their numbed arms with pins and sprigs of rosemary, invoking both madness and holiness to earn some pity and a few coins. "They survive through their miseries by forcing the hands of those with little to spare," Edgar reflected. Inspired, he decided to adopt a similar approach. "Poor Turlygod! Poor Tom! At least they are somebody. Edgar is now nobody," he whispered to himself as he prepared to transform into a figure no one would recognize. With one last look around to ensure he was alone, he vanished deeper into the woods.

SCENE 4

As King Lear approached Gloucester's castle with the Fool and a gentleman by his side, he expressed his disbelief that his own daughters had not sent back his messenger after they had unexpectedly left home.

The gentleman explained, "From what I've gathered, they had no plans to leave the night before."

At that moment, Kent, restrained in stocks, greeted them, "Hail to thee, noble master!"

. . .

King Lear, surprised and a bit upset, asked, "Are you actually finding amusement in this disgrace?"

"Not at all, my lord," Kent replied firmly.

The Fool, always quick to find humor in misfortune, chimed in, "Ha, ha! Look at those cruel garters. It seems horses are tied by their heads, dogs and bears by their necks, monkeys around their midsections, and men by their legs. If a man is too lively with his legs, he ends up in wooden stocks."

King Lear, growing concerned, questioned, "Who would mistake their authority so greatly as to put you here?"

"It was both your son and daughter," Kent revealed.

"No," King Lear denied, unable to believe it.

"Yes, it's true," Kent insisted.

. . .

"No, I tell you."

"I'm telling you, yes."

"No, no, they wouldn't do this."

"But they did," Kent asserted.

King Lear, frustrated and incredulous, swore, "By Jupiter, I swear they wouldn't dare."

Equally adamant, Kent countered, "By Juno, I swear they did."

"They wouldn't dare; they couldn't, they wouldn't do such a thing. It's worse than murder to commit such violent outrage in your name," King Lear raged, seeking an explanation. "Tell me quickly, how could you possibly deserve such treatment, or how could they justify doing this as if it came from me?"

. . .

Kent explained to King Lear, "My lord, when I was at their home, I presented your letters to them. Even before I could rise from my kneeling position, a messenger arrived, exhausted and panting, carrying greetings from Goneril. He delivered his letters despite the interruption, which they read immediately. After reading, they quickly gathered their servants, mounted their horses, and commanded me to follow and wait for their reply. They gave me cold looks. Here, I encountered another messenger, whose reception seemed to undermine mine. He was the same one who had recently insulted you boldly. Frustrated, I confronted him, which caused a commotion. Your son and daughter decided my actions justified this public shaming."

The Fool, listening intently, added his own cryptic observation:

"Winter isn't over if the wild geese fly that way. Fathers in rags may render their children blind, but those with wealth will see their children's kindness. Yet, Fortune, that relentless cheat, never favors the poor. Despite everything, you will face as many sorrows from your daughters as the days in a year."

. . .

King Lear, overwhelmed by his emotions, exclaimed, "Oh, this anguish swells up toward my heart like a tide! Calm down, my climbing sorrow, you belong beneath me! Where is this daughter now?"

Kent answered, "She's here within, with the Earl, sir."

King Lear, agitated, instructed, "Do not follow me; stay here." He then left hastily.

The gentleman, seeking clarity, asked Kent, "Was there no other offense than what you've mentioned?"

"None," Kent confirmed, puzzled by the lack of support from Lear's entourage.

The Fool, seizing another opportunity for a wry comment, said, "If you were put in the stocks just for asking that, you would have deserved it."

Kent, puzzled by the Fool's remarks, asked, "Why do you say that, fool?"

. . .

The Fool, with his typical cryptic wit, responded, "I'll send you to school with an ant to teach you that there's no working in the winter. Everyone who follows their nose is actually led by their eyes, except the blind. And among twenty, there's hardly a nose that can't detect someone stinking. Let go when a great wheel rolls downhill, or it might drag you down too. But if one climbs uphill, let it pull you after. When a wise man gives you better advice, you can return mine to me. I'd prefer only scoundrels to follow my advice, since a fool offers it. The one who serves for profit and follows just for appearances will leave when it starts to rain and leave you in the storm. But I will stay; the fool stays, and lets the wise man flee. The rogue becomes a fool if he runs away; the fool is no rogue, certainly."

Kent, intrigued, asked, "Where did you learn this, fool?"

"Not in the stocks, fool," replied the Fool, with a sly smile.

. . .

Just then, King Lear re-entered the scene with Gloucester, visibly upset. "Deny to speak with me? They claim to be sick? Tired? They've traveled all night? Those are just excuses, the mere images of rebellion. Fetch me a better answer."

Gloucester tried to explain, "My dear lord, you know the fiery nature of the duke; how steadfast and unmovable he is in his decisions."

King Lear, irate and desperate, exclaimed, "Vengeance! Plague! Death! Confusion! Fiery? What quality? Why, Gloucester, I demand to speak with the Duke of Cornwall and his wife!"

"Well, my good lord, I have already informed them," Gloucester responded, trying to calm the king.

"Informed them! Do you understand what I am asking, man?" King Lear pressed, his frustration mounting.

. . .

"Yes, my good lord," Gloucester affirmed, acknowledging the king's urgent request.

King Lear's frustration boiled over as he addressed Gloucester, "The king wishes to speak with Cornwall; the father wants to talk to his daughter and commands her presence. Are they aware of this? My breath and blood! Fiery? The fiery duke? Inform the impetuous duke that—no, wait, perhaps he is unwell. Illness often neglects duties that health obliges us to perform. We aren't ourselves when nature, oppressed, forces the mind to suffer with the body. I'll hold back for now. I've struggled against my more impulsive desires, to accuse the indisposed as though they were healthy. How appalling my situation is! Why should Kent sit here? This act convinces me that the duke and his wife's absence is merely a scheme. Bring me my servant. Go, tell the duke and his wife that I wish to speak with them, immediately. Have them come out and listen to me, or I will stand at their door and beat the drum until it awakens death itself."

Gloucester, hoping for reconciliation, said, "I wish for all to be well between you." He then left to carry out Lear's commands.

. . .

King Lear, trying to calm his surging emotions, murmured, "Oh, my heart, my rising heart! But calm down."

The Fool, always ready with a jest, advised, "Chide it, uncle, as the cook did to the eels when she put them alive in the pie. She smacked them on the head with a stick and shouted, 'Down, you rascals, down!' It was her brother who, out of sheer kindness to his horse, buttered the hay."

Just then, Cornwall, Regan, Gloucester, and their servants entered. King Lear greeted them, "Good morning to you both."

Cornwall responded courteously, "Hail to your grace!"

Kent was then released from his constraints.

. . .

Regan, with a smile, added, "I am glad to see your highness."

King Lear turned his attention to Regan, his voice heavy with emotion, "Regan, I think you care; I have reason to believe so. If you didn't, I'd renounce the connection to your mother's grave, branding her an adulteress."

He then noticed Kent, "Oh, you're free now? We'll talk about that later." Returning his focus to Regan, he continued, "Your sister is cruel, Regan. She has clamped a sharp-toothed unkindness onto me," he gestured towards his heart, "It's hard for me to even speak to you; you wouldn't believe how badly she has treated me."

Regan tried to soothe him, "Please, sir, be patient. I still hold out hope. You might not fully appreciate what she deserves just as she might not fulfill her duties fully."

Curious and somewhat aggrieved, Lear asked, "And how is that?"

. . .

Regan defended her sister, "I can't believe she would neglect her obligations. If she has curbed the excesses of your followers, it was done reasonably and with good intentions, absolving her of any fault."

King Lear's anger flared, "My curses on her!"

Regan cautioned him gently, "Oh, sir, you are old. Nature in you is at its limit; you should be guided by those who can better assess your condition than you can yourself. Therefore, I urge you to reconcile with our sister; admit you've wronged her."

Lear was incredulous, "Ask her forgiveness? Just look at how demeaning this is," he said as he simulated kneeling, "'Dear daughter, I confess I am old; age is a burden: on my knees, I beg you for clothes, a bed, and food.'"

His words dripped with bitterness as he mimicked what he saw as a humiliating plea for basic needs from his own daughter.

. . .

Regan, frustrated with her father's vitriolic outburst, pleaded, "Good sir, no more; these are unsightly actions. Please, go back to my sister."

King Lear, his anger unabated, rose and declared defiantly, "Never, Regan. She has reduced my retinue by half, scowled at me, and lashed out with her words, striking at my heart like a serpent. May all the vengeances of heaven rain down on her ungrateful head! May the very air she breathes make her limbs weak!"

Cornwall, shocked by the intensity of Lear's curses, interjected, "Fie, sir, fie!"

Undeterred, Lear continued his curse, "You swift lightnings, blind her with your flames! Let the mists drawn by the sun infect her beauty and wither her pride!"

. . .

Regan, alarmed by her father's ferocity, exclaimed, "Oh blessed gods! You will wish the same on me when you're in such a mood."

Lear softened slightly, "No, Regan, you will never bear my curse. Your nature is too gentle; you don't harbor the harshness her eyes reveal. Yours bring comfort, not pain. You don't begrudge my pleasures, cut off my followers, trade harsh words, reduce my provisions, or bar my entry. You remember well the duties of kindness and gratitude, the bonds of childhood, the effects of courtesy. You haven't forgotten the half of the kingdom I endowed you with."

"Good sir, let's stick to the matter at hand," Regan tried to steer the conversation.

"Who put my man in the stocks?" Lear demanded, just as a trumpet sounded.

Cornwall questioned, "What's that trumpet sound?"

. . .

Regan recognized it, "It's from my sister, confirming her letter that she would soon be here."

Just then, Oswald entered. King Lear, seeing him, scorned, "This is a lackey, whose borrowed pride relies on the whims of her he serves. Get out, rogue, from my sight!"

Cornwall, noticing King Lear's agitation, inquired, "What do you mean, your grace?"

King Lear, with a blend of hope and accusation, addressed Regan, "Who put my servant in the stocks? Regan, I have good hope you didn't know of this. Who comes here? Oh heavens," he gasped as Goneril entered. He appealed to her, "If you respect old age, if you expect obedience, if you will someday be old, make this your cause; come to my aid!"

Confronting Goneril directly, he asked, "Aren't you ashamed to look upon this beard?" Then, turning to Regan, he pleaded, "Regan, will you support her?"

. . .

Goneril responded, unfazed, "Why shouldn't I take her hand, sir? How have I offended? Not everything you find indiscreet or foolish is actually offensive."

Lear, feeling the physical and emotional strain, exclaimed, "Oh, my body, you are too resilient; will you not break under this strain? How did my servant end up in the stocks?"

Cornwall admitted, "I placed him there, sir. But truly, his own behavior warranted far less leniency."

"You did this?" Lear was incredulous.

Regan, attempting to pacify her father, suggested, "Please, father, accept your weakness as it is. If you agree to return and stay with my sister, dismissing half of your train, then afterwards you can come to me. I am currently away from my home and don't have the means to entertain you."

King Lear, appalled by the suggestion, declared, "Return to her, and dismiss fifty of my men? No, I'd rather renounce all shelter, and brave the hostility of the open air, to become a companion to wolves and owls—enduring the sharp bite of necessity! Return with her? I might as well kneel before the throne of France—who married my youngest without a dowry—and beg like a squire for a pension just to survive. Return with her? You'd do better persuading me to be a slave and packhorse to this detestable servant!" He pointed accusingly at Oswald.

Goneril, indifferent to her father's dramatic refusal, simply stated, "The choice is yours, sir."

King Lear, overwhelmed and pleading, addressed his daughter Regan, "I beg you, daughter, don't drive me to madness. I won't trouble you, my child; farewell. We'll not meet or see one another again. But you are still my flesh, my blood, my daughter; or rather a disease in my flesh, which I must acknowledge as mine. You are a boil, a plague-sore, an inflamed carbuncle in my corrupted blood. But I'll not scold you; let shame come when it will, I do not invoke it. I won't ask the thunder-bearer to strike, nor will I complain about you to the high-judging Jupiter. Mend your ways when you can; improve at your leisure. I can be patient; I can stay with Regan and my hundred knights."

Regan, however, quickly set boundaries, "Not quite so; I wasn't expecting you yet, nor am I prepared to welcome you properly. Listen to my sister; those who mix reason with your passion must accept that you are old, and so—but she knows what she's doing."

King Lear, stunned, asked, "Is this well spoken?"

Regan confidently replied, "I stand by it, sir. What need have you for fifty followers? Isn't that reasonable? Why would you need more, given the expense and risk involved? How can so many people, under two different commands, maintain peace in one house? It's difficult; nearly impossible."

Goneril joined in, suggesting, "Why might not you, my lord, accept service from those she calls servants, or from mine?"

. . .

Regan added, "Why not, my lord? If they fail in their duty, we could intervene. But I see a danger now, and I urge you—if you come to me—bring only twenty-five; I will not accommodate more."

King Lear, feeling betrayed, exclaimed, "I gave you everything—"

"And you gave it at a good time," Regan interjected.

Lear continued, "I made you my guardians, my trustees, but reserved the right to be followed by a certain number of attendants. What, must I come to you with only twenty-five, Regan? Did you say so?"

Regan reaffirmed her stance, "I said it before and I say it again, my lord; no more with me."

King Lear looked between his two daughters, his voice thick with emotion, "Even those considered wicked appear favorable when others are even more so. Not being the worst still places you in some rank of praise." He turned to Goneril, the anger softening slightly, "I'll go with thee; your offer of fifty attendants doubles the twenty-five from her, and it seems you show me twice her love."

Goneril, trying to reason with him, replied, "Hear me, my lord; why do you need twenty-five, ten, or even five followers in a house where there are already twice that many to serve you?"

Regan interjected sharply, "What need for even one?"

King Lear, agitated and hurt, exclaimed, "Oh, do not reason the need! Our basest beggars have excess in the poorest conditions. If we only allow ourselves what nature strictly needs, then life is as cheap as a beast's. You are a lady; if merely being warm were enough, why do you wear finery that hardly keeps you warm? But true need—You heavens, grant me patience, the patience I need! You see me here, you gods, a poor old man, full of grief and burdened by age. If you are stirring my daughters against me, do not let me bear it tamely; fill me with noble anger, and let not the tears of women stain my cheeks! No, you unnatural hags, I will have such revenges on you both, that the whole world shall—I will do such things, what they are, I do not yet know, but they will be the terrors of the earth. You think I'll weep? No, I will not weep. I have full cause to weep, but this heart shall split into a hundred thousand pieces before I weep. Oh fool, I think I shall go mad!"

As Lear's voice rose with his threats, a storm began to brew. He left with Gloucester, Kent, and the Fool, leaving his daughters to contemplate the brewing tempest, both meteorological and emotional.

Cornwall, feeling the change in the atmosphere, suggested, "Let us withdraw; it will be a storm."

Regan, her tone pragmatic yet cold, remarked, "This house is too small; the old man and his people cannot be well accommodated here." The air was tense as they prepared for the storm's full force, mirroring the tempest in Lear's heart.

Goneril remarked with a touch of disdain, "It's his own fault; he has distanced himself from comfort and must now suffer the consequences of his folly."

. . .

Regan agreed, but with conditions, "I'll gladly take him in, but not a single follower."

Goneril nodded, "That's my intention as well. Where is the Earl of Gloucester?"

Cornwall updated them, "He followed the old man out; he has just returned."

Gloucester re-entered, looking concerned. "The king is in high rage."

Cornwall, trying to grasp the situation, asked, "Where is he going?"

"He calls for his horse; but as to where he's heading, I do not know," Gloucester replied, clearly worried.

Cornwall reasoned, "It's best to let him go; he leads himself."

. . .

Goneril quickly added, "My lord, urge him by no means to stay."

Gloucester, aware of the worsening conditions, added his own concerns, "Alas, the night grows dark, and the harsh winds are fiercely blowing; for many miles around, there's scarcely a bush for shelter."

Regan, with a stern philosophy, commented, "Oh sir, to stubborn men, the troubles they bring on themselves must teach them lessons. Close your doors. He is followed by a desperate band, and considering their influence over him, it's wise to be cautious."

Cornwall supported her decision, "Shut your doors, my lord; it's a wild night. Regan advises well; let's stay out of the storm."

They all exited, leaving the stage to the coming tempest, mirroring the turmoil in King Lear's mind and the bleakness of his situation, abandoned by his daughters to the mercy of a cruel storm.

ACT III

SCENE 1

Kent, braving the stormy heath, spotted a familiar face and called out over the howling wind, "Who's there, aside from this awful weather?"

The gentleman, shivering as he replied, matched the chaos of the storm in his mood. "Just a man as troubled as the storm itself."

Recognizing the man, Kent's concern deepened. "I know you. Where is the king?"

. . .

The gentleman gestured towards the tumultuous horizon. "He's out there, wrestling with the storm. He's challenging the winds to sweep the earth into the sea, or to make the waves rise above the shoreline, hoping everything might just vanish or transform. He's tearing at his white hair, which the relentless winds snatch wildly, making him look all the more undone. In his agony, he's trying to outdo the fierce conflict of wind and rain with his own fierce defiance."

"In this dreadful night," the gentleman continued, "even wild beasts that the barest cubs follow would find shelter. Yet, the king runs about unshielded, letting the storm take everything from him."

Kent's worry grew. "But who is with him, keeping him company in such peril?"

"Only his fool," said the gentleman, his voice tinged with sadness. "The fool tries to lighten the king's deep wounds with his jests, but it's a grim task tonight."

. . .

Kent, recognizing the gentleman, seized the moment to confide a crucial message, underpinned by the urgency of their troubled times. "Sir, I know you well, and trust you enough to share a sensitive matter. There's a rift brewing, still hidden by clever disguises, between Albany and Cornwall. Both dukes, like anyone in their high position, have servants who are less what they seem and more akin to spies for France, keen on understanding our state's affairs."

He leaned closer, his voice dropping to ensure only the gentleman could hear. "Indeed, from France, forces are mobilizing towards our fractured kingdom, having already infiltrated some of our key ports, preparing to make their presence known."

Kent's eyes held a serious gleam as he continued, "If you trust my word enough to hasten to Dover, you will find allies grateful for your news on the deep and distressing sorrow that drives the king mad."

"I am a man of integrity and noble heritage," Kent declared, offering a purse. "Take this, and if you encounter Cordelia, show her this ring. She will confirm my identity, which you are yet unaware of. This storm be damned, I must find the king!"

The gentleman, moved by the trust and gravity of Kent's mission, reached out his hand, saying, "Give me your hand; have you nothing more to add?"

Kent clasped his hand firmly, his resolve clear. "Only this — when we locate the king, let's signal to each other. You go one way, I'll go another; whoever finds him first should call out."

With that, they parted ways, each stepping into the tempestuous night with their own heavy burden of purpose.

SCENE 2

As the storm continued to rage across the heath, King Lear and his Fool made their way through the howling winds. Lear, in a burst of defiance against the elements, shouted into the storm, "Let the winds blow and the lightning split the sky! Let the rain drown our church steeples!"

Beside him, the Fool quipped, "Uncle, it's better to have holy water in a dry house than this rain soaking us through. Why don't we go inside and ask for your daughters' blessings? This dreadful night spares no one, wise man or fool alike."

. . .

Lear ignored the suggestion, his voice rising with the tempest, "Keep roaring, storm! I'm not angry at you, elements. I never ruled over you or called you my children, so you owe me nothing. Do your worst; here I am, merely an old man, weak and scorned."

The Fool, ever the source of odd wisdom, countered with a riddle, "Anyone who has a house for his head has a good head on his shoulders. But beware the man who shelters his pride before his reason, for he will find only trouble."

As Lear pondered his next words, a familiar figure approached. It was Kent, disguised but loyal as ever.

"Who's there?" Kent called out into the stormy darkness.

With a smirk, the Fool answered, "A mix of wisdom and folly stands here; that would be a wise man and a fool."

. . .

Kent, finding Lear amidst the tempest, expressed his concern, "Oh sir, you shouldn't be out on such a night. Even creatures that roam the dark are hiding away from this ferocious weather. I've never witnessed such violent storms in my life."

Lear, undeterred and increasingly agitated, called out into the chaos, "Let the gods who oversee this tumult reveal their foes. Those hidden in deceit, harboring dark secrets and crimes, should tremble now!"

Kent, noticing Lear's exposure to the harsh elements, suggested, "My lord, there's a small shelter nearby. It might offer some protection against the storm. Rest there while I confront your daughters, who just denied me entry, and demand some decency from them."

Lear, feeling the effects of the storm and his despair, muttered, "My mind is starting to falter. Come, my boy, are you cold? I feel the chill too. Let's find some shelter."

. . .

The Fool, in his usual blend of wisdom and song, sang about adapting to fortunes, however meager, as they trudged towards the hovel.

Lear, touched by the Fool's songs and perhaps by his own reflections, admitted softly, "True, my good boy. Lead us to this shelter."

As they exited, the Fool stayed behind briefly to comment on the night's irony and to deliver a cryptic prophecy about a time of chaos and reversal, a prophecy from an age yet to come, hinting at a deep unraveling of society before he too followed into the night.

SCENE 3

Gloucester's castle was filled with tension as Gloucester and his son Edmund stepped into the room. Gloucester looked deeply troubled, his brow furrowed with worry. "Oh, Edmund, I don't like how things are being handled. It's all so wrong. When I asked for permission to show some compassion, they restricted my access to my own home. They've warned me under threat of their ongoing displeasure not to speak of him, plead for him, or help him in any way."

Edmund shook his head, his voice heavy with disdain. "That's utterly cruel and unnatural!"

. . .

Gloucester motioned for silence with a weary gesture. "Say nothing more on it. There's a rift between the dukes, and something even more serious than that. I received a letter tonight; it's too dangerous to talk about openly. I've locked it away. The harm being done to the king will not go unanswered. Forces are already mobilizing; we need to support the king. I'll find him and help him secretly. You should keep the duke occupied so he doesn't suspect my absence. If he asks for me, say I'm sick and have gone to bed. Even if it costs me my life—and it might—I must help the king, my old master. Something dire is brewing, Edmund; please, be cautious."

As Gloucester left, Edmund's expression shifted to one of calculated interest. "This restriction on showing courtesy will be something the duke hears about immediately, along with that letter. It seems a just reward, and it could lead to my gain—that which my father loses; nothing less than everything. As the old falls, the young rise." With those ominous words, Edmund too exited, his mind racing with plans.

SCENE 4

As they stood on the stormy heath in front of a shabby hovel, Kent urged King Lear to take shelter inside. "This is the place, my lord. Please, go inside. The harshness of this open night is too much for us to withstand."

King Lear, agitated and distressed, resisted. "Leave me be," he insisted.

"Please, my lord, come inside," Kent persisted.

"Are you trying to break my heart?" Lear snapped.

. . .

"I'd rather break my own," Kent replied earnestly. "Please, come in."

King Lear shook his head, his voice filled with a mixture of rage and sorrow. "You think it's bad that this storm is soaking us to the skin. To you, maybe it is. But I'm dealing with something far worse inside me, making this seem minor. You'd avoid a bear, but if escaping meant facing a raging sea, you'd run right into the bear's jaws. When you're mentally free, your body feels more delicate. This storm inside my mind strips all other sensations away, except the pain it beats into me. The ungratefulness of a child! It's as unnatural as if my own mouth tore at my hand when it tried to feed."

Pausing, his voice heavy with emotion, Lear declared, "But I won't cry anymore. To be locked out on a night like this! Regan, Goneril, your once-kind father who gave everything—no, I must avoid madness. No more thoughts on that."

Again, Kent tried, "Please, my lord, come inside."

. . .

Lear waved him off. "Go in yourself and find some comfort. This storm won't let me stop thinking about things that hurt even more. But alright, I'll go in."

He turned to his Fool, who stood nearby, soaked and shivering. "Go ahead inside, boy. You too, you poor soul with no home—get inside. I'll pray, then sleep."

As the Fool scurried into the hovel, Lear looked out into the storm with a newfound empathy. "Poor naked wretches, wherever you are, enduring this merciless storm, how do you survive with no shelter or food, your clothes barely hanging on you? Oh, I've cared too little for this! Those who live in comfort, step out and feel what these poor souls feel. Maybe then, we can help them and show the heavens that we can be more just."

Inside the hovel, Edgar's voice echoed eerily, "Fathom and half, fathom and half! Poor Tom!" The Fool, spooked, dashed out of the shelter.

. . .

"Don't come in here, uncle! There's a spirit," the Fool cried out to King Lear, his voice trembling. "Help me, help me!"

Kent reached out to steady him. "Give me your hand. Who's there?"

"A spirit, a spirit! He says his name's Poor Tom," the Fool stammered.

Kent peered into the dim interior. "Who are you mumbling in the straw there? Come out!"

Edgar, disguised as a madman, stumbled forward. "Away! The foul fiend follows me! Through the sharp hawthorn, the cold wind howls. Go to your cold bed and warm yourself."

King Lear, observing Edgar's pitiful state, asked him, "Have you given everything to your two daughters? And you ended up like this?"

. . .

Edgar rambled on in his feigned madness, "Who would give anything to poor Tom? The foul fiend has chased me through fire and water, over bog and quagmire. He put knives under my pillow, nooses in my room, poison beside my food. He made me ride a bay horse over narrow bridges, chasing my own shadow as if it were a traitor. Bless your wits! Tom's freezing—O, do de, do de, do de. Save me from whirlwinds, from curses and calamities! Show some charity to poor Tom, tormented by demons. Here, there, everywhere the fiend is after me!"

The storm continued to rage outside as Lear looked on, deeply moved by Edgar's performance. "What? Have his daughters reduced him to this? Couldn't you save anything? Did you give them everything?"

The Fool chimed in, half in jest, "He kept a blanket, else we'd all be utterly disgraced."

King Lear, his wrath reignited by the sight of Edgar's feigned destitution, cursed, "Now may all the plagues that hover in the air above, waiting to punish men's sins, fall upon your daughters!"

. . .

Kent gently corrected King Lear, who was still caught up in his anger and confusion. "He has no daughters, sir."

King Lear, overwhelmed by his own thoughts and emotions, continued, "Death to traitors! Nothing but the cruelty of daughters could bring a man so low. Is it now common that fathers are cast aside with so little compassion by their own children? Such a fitting punishment for me—this flesh created those ungrateful daughters."

Amidst the cold, Edgar chanted nonsensically, perhaps to stay warm or perhaps lost in his act of madness, "Pillicock sat on Pillicock-hill: Halloo, halloo, loo, loo!"

The Fool, shivering, observed wryly, "This cold night will turn us all into fools and madmen."

Edgar, still in character as Poor Tom, continued his warnings, "Beware the foul fiend: obey your parents, keep your promises, don't swear, don't covet another's spouse, don't desire grand clothing. I'm so cold."

King Lear, intrigued, asked Edgar, "What were you before this?"

Edgar replied with a detailed confession of a fabricated past, "I was a servant, proud in heart and mind; I styled my hair, wore fancy clothes, fulfilled my mistress's desires, and sinned in secrecy. I loved wine, gambled with dice, and was more promiscuous than a sultan. False-hearted, easily swayed, violent, lazy, sly, greedy, mad, and predatory. Don't let the allure of material things or women corrupt you. Stay away from brothels, keep your hands to yourself, avoid debt, and resist the devil."

The storm continued as he added cryptically, "Still the cold wind blows through the hawthorn. Says suum, mun, ha, no, nonny. Dolphin my boy, my boy, sessa! let him trot by."

King Lear, moved by Edgar's appearance and the raw elements, lamented the human condition. "You'd be better off dead than enduring this storm naked. Is this what man really is? Think about it. You don't owe anything to luxury, no silk, no leather, no wool, no scent. Look, all of us here are reduced to nothing! We are merely simple, bare creatures without our trappings." In a symbolic gesture, Lear began tearing off his own clothes.

"Prithee, uncle, stay calm; it's a terrible night for a swim," the Fool tried to lighten the mood, "A little fire in this vast field would be like an old man's heart; a tiny spark while the rest of him is cold. Look, here comes a walking fire."

As Gloucester approached with a torch, Edgar pointed at him, deep in his act, "This is the foul fiend Flibbertigibbet: he roams from dusk till dawn, causes diseases, squints eyes, and brings misfortune to the poor and the crops."

He recited an old charm against evil, "St. Withold walked the old grounds three times; he met the nightmare and her nine-fold; commanded her to pledge her truth, and be gone, witch, be gone!"

. . .

Kent, noticing the king's discomfort in the storm, asked with concern, "How are you feeling, Your Grace?"

King Lear, distracted by the presence of another, asked, "Who's that?"

Kent queried the newcomer, "Who's there? What do you seek?"

Gloucester approached, trying to make out the figures in the dark, "Who are you? What are your names?"

Edgar, still disguised as the madman Poor Tom, rattled off a list of his grotesque supposed diet, "Poor Tom; that eats frogs, toads, tadpoles, newts, and drinks from stagnant pools. In his rage, when haunted by demons, he eats cow dung as salad; swallows rats and stray dogs; who's been whipped from place to place, punished and jailed; who once had horses to ride and clothes to wear, but now feeds only on mice and rats, his sustenance for seven long years. Beware my follower. Peace, Smulkin; peace, thou fiend!"

Gloucester, taken aback by Edgar's appearance and ramblings, remarked to Lear, "Your Grace, have you no better company tonight?"

Edgar cryptically replied, "The prince of darkness is a gentleman: Modo he's called, and Mahu."

Gloucester lamented the state of things, "Our own flesh and blood has become so vile, my lord, that it despises its own origins."

Still in character, Edgar shivered, "Poor Tom's a-cold."

Gloucester, ever dutiful, urged them, "Come inside with me. I cannot neglect my duty to obey your daughters' harsh orders, even though they command me to lock my doors against you. Despite the risk, I've come to find you and bring you to warmth and sustenance."

. . .

King Lear, intrigued by Edgar's act, expressed a desire to converse with him first. "Let me speak with this philosopher. What causes thunder?"

Kent, worried about the king's exposure to the harsh elements, advised, "Good my lord, accept his offer; let's go inside."

Lear, however, was drawn to Edgar's mad wisdom. "I want to exchange a few words with this learned Theban. What do you study?"

Edgar responded, still in character, "How to ward off the fiend, and to exterminate pests."

King Lear, deeply engaged by Edgar's guise, requested, "Let me ask you one question in private."

Kent, observing the king's fixation and concern for his safety, suggested, "Once more, urge him to go inside, my lord; his mind begins to falter."

. . .

Gloucester, understanding the gravity of the situation, could not fault the king's distress. Amid the relentless storm, he reflected on his own troubles, "His daughters seek his death. Ah, that good Kent! He predicted this, poor exiled man. You say the king is becoming mad; I tell you, my friend, I am nearly mad myself. I had a son who was recently banished; he even sought my life. I loved him dearly, no father loved his son more. The grief has muddled my mind. What a terrible night this is! I implore you, Your Grace—"

King Lear, momentarily recollecting his manners, replied, "Oh, forgive me, sir. Noble philosopher, stay with us."

Edgar, still embodying Poor Tom, simply muttered, "Tom's a-cold."

Gloucester urged, "Get inside, fellow, into the hovel; keep yourself warm."

. . .

King Lear decided, "Let us all go inside."

"This way, my lord," Kent directed, guiding them toward shelter.

King Lear, still fascinated by Edgar, declared, "I will stay close to my philosopher."

"Please, my lord, humor him; let him take the fellow with him," Kent implored.

Gloucester agreed, "Take him in hand."

"Come on, sir, follow us," Kent urged Edgar.

"Come, good Athenian," King Lear invited, playing along with the pretense.

"No more words: hush," Gloucester cautioned, sensing the tension and the need for calm.

. . .

As they moved to exit the stormy scene, Edgar, lost in his character, recited mysteriously, "Child Rowland to the dark tower came, his word was still, —Fie, foh, and fum, I smell the blood of a British man."

With these cryptic words hanging in the air, they all departed, seeking refuge from the tempest.

SCENE 5

At Gloucester's castle, Cornwall and Edmund stepped into a secluded room. Cornwall, with a steely look in his eye, vowed, "I will have my revenge before I leave this house."

Edmund, conflicted and cautious, responded, "My lord, I'm worried about how this might look. My loyalty overriding my natural instincts... it's troubling."

Cornwall, seeing the uncertainty in Edmund, clarified, "It's not just your brother's malice that drove him to seek death. He was pushed by his own flaws, provoked by his deserving qualities."

Edmund, clutching a letter, lamented, "How cruel my fate is that I must regret being just! This letter he mentioned confirms his involvement with France. If only this treason hadn't come to light, or I hadn't been the one to uncover it!"

Cornwall urged, "Come with me to the duchess."

"If the contents of this paper are true, we have significant matters to attend to," Edmund noted, weighing the severity of the situation.

"Whether true or not, it has made you the Earl of Gloucester. Now, find your father to ensure he's ready to be apprehended," Cornwall commanded.

Alone for a moment, Edmund whispered to himself, "If I find him with the king, it will only deepen his suspicions. Yet, I must continue to show my loyalty, even though it clashes with my own family ties."

. . .

Cornwall, placing his trust in Edmund, promised, "Rely on me, and you will find in me a love deeper than any father's."

With that, they left the room to carry out their plans.

SCENE 6

In a modest room of a farmhouse near the castle, Gloucester welcomed King Lear, Kent, the Fool, and Edgar. "This is better than being outside," Gloucester said, grateful for the shelter. "I'll make it more comfortable as best I can and won't be away long."

Kent responded, appreciating Gloucester's efforts. "He's lost control because of his impatience. May the gods thank you for your kindness!" After saying this, Gloucester left the room.

. . .

Edgar, caught up in his delusions, muttered to himself. "Frateretto tells me Nero fishes in a dark lake. Be pure, stay innocent, and avoid evil."

The Fool, trying to lighten the mood, asked King Lear, "Uncle, tell me, is a madman a gentleman or a commoner?"

"A king! A king!" Lear exclaimed, his mind adrift in madness.

"No," the Fool joked, "he's a commoner who has a gentleman for a son. That's real madness, seeing your son surpass you in status."

Lear, agitated and rambling, cried out, "Imagine a thousand fiery spears piercing them!"

Edgar groaned, feeling tormented. "The evil spirit gnaws at my back."

. . .

"The man who trusts a wild wolf, a horse's health, a boy's love, or a prostitute's promise is truly mad," the Fool declared, echoing the chaos around them.

Lear, caught up in his own justice, commanded, "It shall be done; I'll put them on trial right away." He pointed to Edgar. "Come, sit here, you wise judge." Then to the Fool, "And you, wise man, sit here. Now, let's deal with these villains!"

Edgar looked around wildly. "See how he glares at us!"

"Do you need eyes to judge, madam?" he called out as if to an unseen figure. "Cross over, Bessy, come to me."

The Fool sang a little rhyme:
 "Her boat has a leak,
 And she must not speak
 Why she dares not come over to thee."

. . .

Edgar, caught in his hallucinations, continued, "The evil spirit haunts poor Tom with a nightingale's voice. Hopdance cries in Tom's belly for two white herrings. Don't croak, dark angel; I have no food for you."

Kent approached Edgar with concern. "How are you, sir? Don't look so shocked. Why don't you lie down and rest for a bit?"

King Lear, however, was focused on other matters. "First, I want to see their trial. Bring in the evidence." He directed Edgar, "You, dressed as a man of justice, take your place," and then to the Fool, "You, his partner in fairness, sit beside him." Turning to Kent, he added, "You're part of this commission too, take a seat."

Edgar, playing along in his confused state, declared, "Let's be just." Then, slipping further into his delusion, he asked, "Are you awake, cheerful shepherd? Your sheep are in the corn. Just one blow from your tiny mouth, and they'll be safe. Ah, the cat is gray."

. . .

King Lear, caught up in his delusions of holding a trial, announced, "First to be tried is Goneril. I swear before you all, she abused her poor father, the king."

The Fool, entering into the play-acting, called out, "Come here, mistress. Is your name Goneril?"

King Lear insisted, "She cannot deny it."

The Fool, mocking the situation, said, "I apologize, I mistook you for a stool."

King Lear, increasingly agitated, pointed out another imaginary adversary. "And here's another, her appearance reveals her corrupt heart. Stop her! Arms, arms, sword, fire! Corruption is everywhere! Why has justice failed to stop her?"

Edgar, trying to soothe the tense atmosphere, blessed Kent, "Bless your sharp senses!"

. . .

Kent, seeing Lear's distress, lamented, "Oh, pity! Where is that patience you so often boasted about?"

Edgar, whispering to himself, realized, "My tears are starting to sympathize with him; they'll ruin my act."

King Lear, growing more distraught, cried out, "Even the little dogs, Tray, Blanch, and Sweet-heart, they're all barking at me."

Edgar, still in character as 'Poor Tom', threatened, "Tom will scare them off. No matter if a dog's mouth is black or white, if its tooth bites, it poisons. Whether mastiff, greyhound, mongrel, hound, spaniel, or any other, Tom will make them cry. By tossing my head like this, I'll scare them all away."

He continued his manic chant, "Do de, de, de. Sessa! Let's go, march to the festivals, fairs, and markets. Poor Tom, your horn is dry."

King Lear, still caught in his feverish state, suggested, "Then let them dissect Regan; see what's within her heart. What in nature could possibly harden their hearts so?"

Addressing Edgar, he added, "You, I'll keep as one of my hundred knights, but I don't like the style of your clothes. You might claim they are Persian, but they need changing."

Kent, concerned for Lear's wellbeing, urged, "Now, my lord, please rest here for a while."

"Make no noise, draw the curtains," Lear whispered, his mind wandering. "We'll go to supper in the morning."

The Fool quipped, "And I'll go to bed at noon."

At that moment, Gloucester re-entered the room. "Where is the king, my master?" he asked urgently.

Kent replied, "Here, sir; but please don't disturb him, he's lost his senses."

. . .

Gloucester quickly moved to action. "My friend, please, lift him in your arms. I've overheard a plot to kill him. There's a carriage ready; put him in it, and hurry to Dover. There you'll find safety and a welcome. If you delay even half an hour, his life, yours, and all who try to defend him will be at risk. Hurry, follow me; I'll lead you to safety."

As Kent prepared to move Lear, he reflected, "Nature needs rest. This sleep could have soothed your shattered senses, if only there were time."

He then called to the Fool, "Come, help carry your master; you can't stay here."

"Let's hurry," Gloucester urged, and they all exited, leaving Edgar alone.

In solitude, Edgar mused on the human condition. "When we see our betters suffer the same as us, our own troubles seem less daunting. Suffering alone is the harshest; it's easier when shared. Now, seeing the king brought low like this, my own troubles seem lighter. He suffers as a father, as I suffer as a son. Now, I must be cautious and reveal myself only when the time is right to correct false judgments about me. For tonight, my hope is merely for the king's safe escape. I must stay hidden."

With that, Edgar slipped away into the shadows.

SCENE 7

In the austere halls of Gloucester's castle, Cornwall, Regan, Goneril, Edmund, and their servants gathered with a sense of urgency. Cornwall directed one of the servants, his voice firm and commanding, "Quickly, send word to your master; give him this letter. The French forces have landed. And find Gloucester, that traitor."

As some servants hurried away on their tasks, Regan's voice cut through the air, sharp and merciless, "Hang him at once."

Goneril, equally ruthless, added, "And gouge out his eyes."

. . .

Cornwall waved a dismissive hand, indicating the matter was already settled in his mind. "Leave him to me. Edmund, stay with our sister. The actions we must take against your father are too harsh for your eyes. Inform the duke of your destination and urge him to ready his forces quickly. We must do the same. Let's keep each other informed swiftly." He then bid farewell to his companions with a touch of warmth that belied the coldness of his orders, "Farewell, dear sister, and you too, Lord Gloucester."

Just then, Oswald burst into the room, urgency apparent in his demeanor. "Where is the king?"

Cornwall's interest piqued immediately. "Where's the king?" echoed Cornwall, his interest piqued.

Oswald quickly reported, "Lord Gloucester has helped him escape. About thirty-six of his knights, all fiercely loyal, intercepted him at the gate. Along with a few lords, they've accompanied him towards Dover, where he claims allies await."

. . .

Cornwall turned sharply to his remaining servants. "Prepare horses for your mistress," he ordered, his mind already racing with the implications of this news.

Goneril bid a quick farewell, "Farewell, sweet lord and sister," and along with Edmund and Oswald, she exited.

Once they were gone, Cornwall's voice was like steel as he commanded the remaining servants, "Find the traitor Gloucester, tie him up like a common thief, and bring him here."

As they departed to carry out his orders, Cornwall reflected aloud, though more to himself, "Though we must adhere to the forms of justice before taking his life, our authority will certainly expedite our revenge. And while some may criticize, they cannot stop us."

Moments later, Gloucester was dragged in by the servants, struggling against his binds. Regan spat out, scorn lining her face, "You ungrateful fox! It's him."

Cornwall approached the bound man, his voice cold as he ordered, "Tie his arms tightly." The castle's air, once filled with the rustle of hurried movements and whispered plots, now settled into a heavy, ominous quiet.

Gloucester, bound and helpless, looked around at the stern faces surrounding him and pleaded, "What do you mean by this? Please, remember you are guests in my home. Don't treat me unfairly."

Cornwall ignored his pleas and commanded the servants, "Tie him to the chair."

As they secured him, Regan accused him venomously, "Tighter, tighter! Oh, you filthy traitor!"

Gloucester protested, his voice filled with indignation, "Cruel lady, I am no traitor."

. . .

Cornwall, unmoved, simply repeated, "Tie him to that chair. You'll see what you're in for, villain."

Regan, in her anger, yanked at Gloucester's beard. He cried out, "By the gods, it's disgraceful to treat me this way, pulling at my beard!"

Regan sneered at the white hairs in her hand, "So white, and yet so traitorous!"

Gloucester rebuked her, "Shame on you, lady. These hairs you pull from me will come back to accuse you. I am your host. You shouldn't manhandle me like common thieves. What are you planning to do?"

Ignoring his questions, Cornwall interrogated him about his recent correspondences, "What letters have you recently received from France?"

Regan cut in, "Just give us a straightforward answer; we already know the truth."

. . .

Cornwall continued the questioning, pressing him further, "And what dealings do you have with the traitors who have recently entered our kingdom?"

Regan added, "Where did you send the mad king? Tell us."

Gloucester, maintaining a semblance of calm, replied, "I wrote a letter based on information from a neutral party, not an enemy."

Cornwall scoffed, "Cunning."

Regan chimed in, "And deceitful."

Cornwall pressed him further, his tone sharp, "Where have you sent the king?"

"Towards Dover," Gloucester answered simply.

. . .

Regan demanded, "Why to Dover? Weren't you ordered not to do so at your own risk?"

Cornwall echoed her, pressing for clarity, "Why Dover? Answer that first." The room tightened with tension, awaiting Gloucester's response.

Bound and helpless, Gloucester faced his accusers with grim acceptance. "I am tied to the stake, and I must endure whatever comes," he declared solemnly.

Regan, relentless, pressed further, "Why Dover? Tell us."

Gloucester, his voice tinged with despair and defiance, replied, "Because I could not bear to see you, with your cruel hands, gouge out his poor old eyes; nor could I watch your sister, fierce as she is, tear at his sacred flesh. Even the stormy sea would have risen to protect him on that dark and terrible night, supporting him against the fierce elements. Yet, despite his sufferings, he helped the heavens to bring rain. If wolves had howled outside your door during such cruel times, you should have locked them out, showing at least that mercy. But I believe divine vengeance will catch up to such cruel children as yourselves."

Cornwall's response was cold and merciless. "You will never see it happen." Turning to the servants, he ordered, "Hold him down in the chair. I will crush his eyes beneath my feet."

Gloucester, sensing the impending brutality, cried out in desperation, "Anyone who hopes to grow old, help me now! Oh, this is cruel! Oh, gods!"

Regan mocked the unfolding drama, "One side mocks the other; and so does the other."

Cornwall, intent on carrying out his gruesome task, sneered, "If you expect to see vengeance—"

Suddenly, a servant intervened, his voice urgent and bold. "My lord, hold! I've served you since I was a child; never have I done you a greater service than I do now in urging you to stop."

Regan lashed out at the servant's audacity, "How dare you, you cur!"

The servant stood firm, his courage unwavering. "If you had a beard, I'd shake it in your face for this quarrel. What do you mean by this cruelty?"

Cornwall, enraged, called him a villain and drew his sword. The servant faced him bravely, "Then come on, and let anger decide this."

Regan, driven by fury, grabbed a sword and attacked the servant from behind, shouting, "A peasant dares to stand up like this!"

The servant, mortally wounded, fell, his last words to Gloucester a plea, "My lord, you have one eye left to witness some justice on him. Oh!" With that, he died.

. . .

Cornwall, determined to complete his vile act, declared, "Lest it see more, prevent it. Out, vile jelly!" And with that, he gouged out Gloucester's eye.

Gloucester, thrust into darkness, cried out in agony, "All is dark and comfortless. Where is my son Edmund? Edmund, stir up all that is human within you, to stop this monstrous deed."

Regan scorned Gloucester as he called out for his son, "Out, treacherous villain! You cry for him who despises you. It was Edmund who revealed your treasons to us; he's too noble to pity you."

Realizing his tragic error, Gloucester lamented, "Oh, my mistakes! Then Edgar was wrongly accused. Kind gods, forgive me for that and protect him!"

Regan, unmoved by his pleas, ordered, "Throw him out of the gates, and let him find his way to Dover by scent alone."

. . .

One of the servants led the blinded Gloucester away, leaving him to his fate.

Turning to Cornwall, who was also wounded in the scuffle, Regan asked, "How are you, my lord? How do you look?"

Cornwall, feeling the impact of his injury, replied, "I've been hurt. Follow me, lady." He then commanded, "Turn out that eyeless villain; toss that slave onto the dunghill. Regan, I'm bleeding quickly. This injury is badly timed; give me your arm."

Cornwall and Regan then exited, with her supporting him.

Left behind, the servants expressed their horror and disillusionment at the brutality they had witnessed. One remarked darkly, "I'll never care about committing evil deeds if this man comes to any good."

. . .

Another voiced a bleak prophecy, "If she lives long and dies a natural death, it will turn all women into monsters."

A third servant suggested, "Let's follow the old earl and find the madman to guide him where he wishes. His madness seems to welcome any ally."

The first servant decided to take immediate action, "You go ahead; I'll get some flax and egg whites to help stop his bleeding. Now, may heaven help him!"

They dispersed, each to their tasks, shaken by the day's grim events.

ACT IV

SCENE 1

Edgar walked onto the heath, wrestling with his thoughts. "It's better to be despised and known than flattered and still despised. Even the most unfortunate, the lowest of the low, still hold onto hope and live without fear. The saddest part is falling from the best to the worst, yet even the worst situations can eventually turn into laughter. So, I welcome you, intangible air that I now embrace! The misery you've blown my way leaves me owing nothing to your storms."

Just then, he noticed someone approaching. It was his father, Gloucester, led by an old man. Edgar was stunned. "My father, led so poorly? Oh, the world is cruel indeed. If it weren't for your harsh changes, life would easily succumb to old age."

The old man spoke, "Oh, my good lord, I've been a tenant to you and your father for eighty years."

Gloucester, feeling overwhelmed, dismissed him, "Go away, leave me be. Your attempts to comfort me are useless; they might even harm you."

"But sir, you cannot see your path," the old man insisted gently.

"I don't need a path because I have no eyes to see one," Gloucester responded bitterly. "When I had my sight, I still stumbled. Often our possessions make us complacent, and our very lacks turn out to be valuable. Oh, Edgar, my son, you are the victim of your father's fury. If only I could touch you again, I would feel as if I could see."

The old man, confused by the sounds around him, asked, "Who's there?"

. . .

Edgar, hidden nearby and overhearing all, thought to himself, "Can anyone really say they've hit rock bottom? I'm worse off than ever before."

The old man recognized the voice, though distorted, "It's poor mad Tom."

Edgar kept his thoughts to himself, reflecting on his plight, "And I might sink even lower yet. The worst hasn't come as long as we can say, 'This is the worst.'"

The old man questioned the newcomer, "Where are you headed?"

Gloucester, uncertain, asked, "Is that a beggar-man?"

"Both a madman and a beggar," the old man clarified.

. . .

Gloucester reflected, "He must have some reason if he can beg. Last night's storm brought to mind such a wretched soul, and it made me think of my son. My thoughts were hardly kind toward him then, but I've learned more since. We are like insects to playful boys to the gods; they kill us for their amusement."

Edgar, overhearing this and keeping to himself, thought, "Why must it be this way? It's a cruel role, being the fool in the face of grief, stirring both one's own anger and that of others." He then called out, without revealing his identity, "Bless you, master!"

"Is that the man without clothes?" Gloucester inquired.

"Yes, my lord," the old man confirmed.

"Then please, leave us for now," Gloucester requested. "If you care to help, find us a mile or two towards Dover, out of goodwill from old times. Bring something to cover this poor, naked man who I will ask to guide me."

. . .

"Sir, he is not in his right mind," the old man worried.

"It's the curse of these times; madmen lead the blind. Follow my instructions, or do as you see fit. But above all, leave us," Gloucester insisted.

The old man agreed, "I'll bring the best clothing I have, come what may," and then he left.

Gloucester turned to Edgar, "Sirrah, you, the man with no clothes—"

Edgar, shivering and still in his role, muttered to himself, "Poor Tom's cold. I can't keep up this disguise much longer."

"Come here, fellow," Gloucester called to him.

Edgar muttered to himself, aware of the part he had to maintain, "And yet I must continue. Bless your kind eyes, they bleed."

. . .

Gloucester, unaware of Edgar's true identity, asked him, "Do you know the way to Dover?"

Edgar replied, his voice tinged with feigned madness, "Every way—stile and gate, horse path and footpath. Poor Tom has been terrified out of his senses; bless you, son of a good man, from the evil spirits! Five demons have tormented poor Tom at once—lust, silence, theft, murder, and bizarre grimaces that now plague chambermaids and servants. So, bless you, master!"

Gloucester, moved by Edgar's apparent wretchedness, offered him a purse. "Here, take this purse, you who have been beaten down by the heavens themselves. My misery makes you the more fortunate. May the heavens continue to act this way! Let those stuffed with excess, who ignore the laws and feel nothing because they suffer nothing, quickly feel the heavens' force. Thus, excess would be undone, and everyone would have enough. Do you know the way to Dover?"

. . .

"Yes, master," Edgar confirmed.

"There's a cliff there, towering and bending over the sea," Gloucester described. "Just lead me to the very edge of it, and I will alleviate the burdens you carry with the wealth I possess. From there, I won't need any further guidance."

"Give me your arm," Edgar offered. "Poor Tom will lead you."

Together, they exited, Edgar leading Gloucester towards an uncertain destiny.

SCENE 2

Scene II. Before Albany's palace.

Goneril and Edmund enter.

Goneril greets him warmly, "Welcome, my lord. I'm surprised our gentle husband hasn't met us on the way."

Oswald enters.

. . .

Goneril quickly asks, "Now, where's your master?"

Oswald responds with concern, "Madam, he's inside, but he's completely changed. I told him about the army that has landed; he merely smiled. When I mentioned that you were on your way, his only response was 'The worse.' I also spoke of Gloucester's betrayal and his son's loyal service, and he dismissed me as a fool, saying I got everything backwards. It seems what he should dislike pleases him, and what he should like, he finds repulsive."

To Edmund, Goneril declares, "Then you mustn't go any further. It's the cowardly fear in his spirit; he dares not act. He won't respond to offenses. Our hopes for this journey might still come to pass. Edmund, return to my brother; speed up his preparations and lead his forces. I need to take charge here at home and hand over the lesser duties to my husband. This trustworthy servant will relay messages between us. Soon, if you're bold enough to act on your own, you'll receive a command from a mistress. Take this token, and spare your words."

. . .

She hands him a token, her tone softening, "Lower your head. This kiss," she whispers, pressing her lips briefly to the token, "if it could speak, would lift your spirits high. Remember this, and farewell."

Edmund, moved, replies solemnly, "Yours, even to the death."

"My most dear Gloucester," Goneril says as Edmund exits.

"Oh, how different one man is from another! To you, a woman owes her service, while a fool takes my place," she muses aloud.

Oswald interrupts, "Madam, the lord is coming."

He exits just as Albany enters.

Goneril, under her breath, remarks bitterly, "I used to be valued."

. . .

Albany confronts Goneril with harsh words, "Oh, Goneril! You're not worth the dust that the harsh wind blows in your face. I'm worried about your cruel nature. A person who rejects their own roots is uncertain at core. A tree that cuts off its branches from its life source will inevitably perish."

Goneril dismisses him sharply, "Enough; your accusations are senseless."

Albany continues, undeterred, "To the corrupt, even wisdom and goodness appear foul. What have you done? You behave like beasts, not daughters. You've driven mad a kind, old man, respected more than you could understand. How could my brother let you do this? A prince who has done so much for you! If the heavens don't intervene to correct these terrible deeds, we will destroy ourselves from within, like monsters of the deep."

Goneril snaps back, calling him a "Coward! You take blows and suffer wrongs without standing up for your honor. You can't even see the difference between honor and suffering. You pity villains before they can cause harm. Where is your courage?

France is invading our land quietly, their leader threatening us, while you, the moral fool, do nothing but wonder why."

Albany retorts, "Look at yourself, devil! Even demons don't show such grotesque deformity as a woman like you."

Goneril mocks him, "Oh, what a pointless fool!"

Albany, seething with anger, warns her, "You deceitful creature, don't turn yourself into a monster. If I were to act on my anger, my hands are ready to tear you apart, but you are still protected by your guise as a woman."

As Goneril challenges Albany's masculinity, their heated exchange is interrupted by the arrival of a messenger.

Albany, looking anxious, quickly asks, "What news?"

. . .

The messenger brings grim tidings, "Oh, my lord, the Duke of Cornwall is dead, killed by his own servant while he was about to gouge out Gloucester's other eye."

Shocked, Albany repeats, "Gloucester's eye!"

The messenger explains further, "A servant, whom he had raised, overcome with guilt, stood against the act and turned his sword on his master. Enraged, Cornwall attacked him, and in the ensuing struggle, the servant killed him, though not without receiving a fatal wound himself."

Albany, reflecting on the justice of the situation, remarks, "This shows that the powers above quickly avenge our earthly crimes. But, oh, poor Gloucester! Did he lose his other eye?"

"Yes, both, my lord," confirms the messenger. He then hands a letter to Goneril, adding, "This letter, madam, demands a swift reply; it's from your sister."

. . .

Goneril, pondering to herself, sees an opportunity, "I like this news in one way; but being a widow, and Gloucester now with my sister, might destroy all that I have planned. Yet, this news isn't entirely unwelcome." She decides to retreat to read and respond to the letter.

Albany, still focused on the tragic events, asks, "Where was Gloucester's son when they took his eyes?"

The messenger informs him, "He was here with my lady."

Albany, puzzled, says, "He is not here now."

"No, my lord; I saw him on his way back," the messenger clarifies.

Albany seeks further clarification, "Does he know about these atrocities?"

. . .

"Yes, my lord. It was he who reported them, and he left the house to ensure the punishment could proceed unhindered."

Albany, resolute, declares, "Gloucester, I live to thank you for the loyalty you showed the king, and to avenge your suffering. Come, tell me more that you know."

They exit together, Albany eager to learn more and determine his course of action.

SCENE 3

Kent met a gentleman in the French camp near Dover, curious about the abrupt return of the King of France to his homeland. "Do you know why the King of France has hurried back so suddenly?" Kent asked.

"It seems he had left some urgent matters unresolved back home," the gentleman explained. "The situation escalated in his absence, threatening the kingdom with great fear and danger, necessitating his immediate return."

"And who is commanding the forces here in his absence?" Kent inquired further.

. . .

"The Marshal of France, Monsieur La Far, has been left in charge," the gentleman replied.

Kent, shifting the topic, asked, "Did the queen show any reaction to the letters I sent?"

"Yes, sir," the gentleman nodded. "She read them in front of me. Tears rolled down her cheeks now and then. It was clear she tried to control her emotions, but the sadness occasionally overpowered her restraint."

"That touched her, then," Kent noted, sensing the impact of his words.

"Indeed, but she remained composed," the gentleman continued. "Her expression was a mix of sadness and patience, like seeing both sunshine and rain at the same time. Her smile was gentle, yet her eyes betrayed her grief, shedding tears as if they were precious stones."

. . .

Kent pondered this for a moment then asked, "Did she say anything?"

"Only a few words, but filled with emotion," the gentleman recalled. "She gasped the word 'father' as if it weighed on her heart. She also cried out 'Sisters! Shame of ladies! What, in the storm? In the night? Let pity not be believed!' After that, she couldn't contain her tears any longer and left to mourn in solitude."

Kent nodded, understanding the depth of her sorrow, as they continued their discussion amidst the uneasy backdrop of the camp.

Kent looked up at the stars as he spoke to the gentleman. "It must be the stars above that shape our lives, for how else could the same parents have children who turn out so differently?" He paused before asking, "Have you spoken to her recently?"

"No," the gentleman replied.

. . .

"Was it before the king returned?" Kent asked.

"No, since his return," the gentleman clarified.

Kent nodded, his thoughts heavy. "The poor, distressed King Lear is in town. Sometimes he's lucid and remembers our purpose here, but he absolutely refuses to see his daughter, Cordelia."

The gentleman, puzzled, asked, "Why is that, sir?"

Kent sighed. "He is overwhelmed by a profound sense of shame. His past unkindness, stripping Cordelia of her blessings and leaving her vulnerable to the cruelty of her sisters, haunts him. These memories inflict such pain that he can't bear to face her."

"That's truly sad," the gentleman sympathized.

"Have you heard about the forces gathering under Albany and Cornwall?" Kent switched topics.

. . .

"Yes, I've heard they are mobilizing," the gentleman confirmed.

"Very well, I will take you to our master Lear and leave you to look after him," Kent proposed. "I need to keep a low profile for a while, but when the time is right, you'll understand my actions. For now, please come with me."

With that, Kent and the gentleman left to find King Lear, each absorbed in their own thoughts about the troubled monarch and the turbulent times surrounding them.

SCENE 4

Cordelia, accompanied by her doctor and soldiers, marched into the tent with a sense of urgency. The sight of her father wandering in madness had shaken her deeply. "It's heartbreaking," she said. "I just saw him, shouting as wildly as a stormy sea, his head crowned with all kinds of wild weeds like nettles and cuckoo-flowers that grow in the fields of our crops."

She quickly commanded one of her officers, "Take a group and comb every part of the high fields. Find him and bring him here to me." As the officer left to carry out her orders, she pondered the challenge of healing a mind so deeply wounded.

. . .

Turning to her doctor, she asked, "Is there any way to restore his sanity?" The doctor replied, "Yes, madam. Rest is often the best medicine for the mind, something he desperately needs. There are many natural remedies that can ease his suffering and close the painful eyes of his distress."

Filled with hope, Cordelia prayed aloud, "All the hidden virtues of the earth, rise with my tears! Help and heal this good man's pain! We must find him quickly before his unchecked rage destroys him."

At that moment, a messenger rushed in with news that British forces were advancing towards them. Cordelia responded calmly, "We knew they were coming and we are ready for them. Oh, my dear father, helping you is my only concern. That's why I'm here, and why France supports me in my grief. We're not driven by ambition, but by love, dear love, and our father's rightful claim."

With a heavy heart yet hopeful spirit, she concluded, "May I soon hear of and see him safe and sound!" With that, she and her retinue prepared to face the incoming challenges, her thoughts always with her father.

SCENE 5

Regan entered Gloucester's castle alongside Oswald. Without delay, she questioned him, "Has my brother already deployed his forces?"

"Yes, madam," Oswald replied promptly.

"And is he there in person?"

"Indeed, madam, though it was a struggle. Your sister proves to be the more formidable leader."

. . .

Regan, growing more concerned, pressed on. "Did Lord Edmund not meet with your lord at home?"

"No, madam."

Regan frowned, pondering the implications. "What could my sister's letter to him possibly mean?"

"I'm not sure, lady."

Regan shook her head, disappointment lacing her tone. "Edmund left in haste on urgent matters. It was foolish to spare Gloucester, blind as he is. Wherever he goes, he stirs people against us. I believe Edmund has left to end his misery and to scout out the enemy's strength."

"I must follow him soon with my letter," Oswald informed her, his tone urgent.

"Our forces will march tomorrow. You should stay; the roads are perilous."

. . .

"I can't, madam," Oswald insisted. "My duty in this business was charged by my lady."

Regan eyed him suspiciously. "Why write to Edmund? Couldn't you just relay her message verbally? There must be something more. Let me see the letter."

Reluctantly, Oswald protested, "Madam, I'd rather not—"

Regan cut him off sharply, "Your lady doesn't love her husband; that much is clear. She had eyes only for Edmund when she was here. I know you're close to her."

Caught off guard, Oswald could only muster a weak, "I, madam?"

"I'm certain of it," Regan affirmed, handing him a note. "Listen, Edmund and I have talked since my husband's death. Edmund is more suited to me now. If you find him, give him this note. And tell your mistress to think carefully on her next steps."

As Regan prepared to leave, she added, "If you happen to hear anything about that traitor Gloucester, remember that those who deal with him will be rewarded."

"I wish I could meet him, madam," Oswald said, his voice low but determined. "I'd prove my loyalty."

Regan nodded, her expression stern. "Take care," she said, and with that, they parted ways.

SCENE 6

In the open fields near Dover, Gloucester and Edgar, who was disguised as a peasant, were walking together.

"When will we reach the top of that hill?" Gloucester asked, looking ahead.

"You're climbing it right now," Edgar replied, his eyes scanning the steep slope. "Feel how hard we're working to get up this hill."

Gloucester paused, feeling the ground under his feet. "It seems flat to me."

. . .

"It's incredibly steep," Edgar said, listening intently. "Can you hear the sea from here?"

"No, I can't," Gloucester admitted.

"That's because your other senses are weakening from the pain your eyes have suffered," Edgar explained.

"That might be true," Gloucester agreed, pondering. "Your voice sounds different; you're speaking more clearly than before."

"You're mistaken; nothing about me has changed except for my clothes," Edgar assured him.

"It seems like you speak more eloquently now," Gloucester observed.

. . .

"Let's stop here," Edgar instructed as they reached a particular spot. "Be careful. It's terrifying and dizzying to look down from here." He described the scene below where tiny birds in the middle of the air looked as small as beetles. "There's someone down there picking samphire, a dangerous job. From here, he looks as small as his head. The fishermen on the beach look like mice, and that large ship anchored out there seems as small as its boat, which itself looks like a mere buoy. The sound of the waves churning the countless pebbles on the shore can't be heard from up here."

Gloucester felt a chill as he listened. "I don't want to look anymore; it might make me dizzy and confused," he said, his voice tinged with fear.

"Stand where I am standing," Edgar offered.

"Give me your hand," Edgar said, guiding Gloucester closer. "You are just a foot away from the very edge. I wouldn't jump from here for anything in the world."

. . .

"Let go of my hand," Gloucester said, pulling his hand away. He handed Edgar another purse, this one containing a valuable jewel. "Take this, it's well worth it for someone in need. May the gods bless you with good fortune! Now, step back, say goodbye, and let me hear you walk away."

"Goodbye, sir, and take care," Edgar responded sincerely.

"With all my heart," Gloucester returned the sentiment.

Edgar pondered to himself, "Why am I playing these games with his despair? It's all to help him overcome it."

Gloucester, kneeling, looked up to the heavens, "O mighty gods! I renounce this world before you, and patiently let go of my immense suffering. If I could endure it longer without questioning your supreme wills, my insignificant and hated existence would just burn out. Oh, if Edgar survives, bless him! Now, farewell." He then let himself fall forward.

. . .

Edgar, watching the scene unfold, exclaimed softly, "He's gone, farewell." He continued to himself, "Yet, it's strange how imagination can drain the life out of us when life itself gives in to such fantasies. If he were truly where he thought he was, he would be gone by now. Is he alive or dead?" Calling out, "Hey, you there! Can you hear me? Speak!"

Gloucester, though expected to be severely hurt, showed signs of stirring. "What are you, sir?"

"Go away, and let me die," Gloucester muttered weakly.

"If you were nothing but air, feathers, or something equally light, falling from such a height would have shattered you like an egg. But here you are, breathing, unharmed, not bleeding, and able to speak. The height you fell from doesn't even compare to the height of ten ship masts; your survival is nothing short of a miracle. Speak to me again," Edgar urged him.

. . .

"But did I actually fall?" Gloucester asked, bewildered.

"You fell from the high edge of this chalk cliff," Edgar explained. "Look up; the lark soaring so high can neither be seen nor heard from here. Just look up."

"Alas, I have no eyes," Gloucester lamented, a deep sadness in his voice. "Is it such a curse to be miserable that even death denies me its escape? It used to be some comfort when suffering could trick a tyrant's anger and thwart his desires."

"Here, take my arm, let me help you up," Edgar offered gently, guiding him to stand. "How do you feel? Can you feel your legs? You're standing."

"Too well, too well," Gloucester muttered, feeling the solid earth beneath him.

"This is beyond all strangeness," Edgar mused, his thoughts racing. "Back on the cliff's edge, what was that creature that left you?"

. . .

"A poor, unfortunate beggar," Gloucester replied.

"From down here, it looked monstrous," Edgar described, his imagination vivid with the terror. "It had eyes as large as moons and a thousand noses, horns twisted and wavy like the rough sea. It must have been some demon; therefore, you should feel fortunate, thinking the gods have spared you for something impossible for men."

Gloucester considered Edgar's words. "I remember now. From this point on, I'll endure my suffering until it cries out 'Enough, enough,' and ends itself. That creature you described, I thought it was a man; it often cried out 'The fiend, the fiend!' and led me to that place."

"Keep your thoughts free and patient," Edgar counseled just as another figure approached.

King Lear entered, oddly dressed in wild flowers, looking every part the mad king he had become.

. . .

"They can't accuse me of counterfeiting; I am the king himself," Lear declared, lost in his delusion.

"Oh, what a heart-wrenching sight!" Edgar exclaimed, seeing the king in such a state.

"Nature triumphs over craftsmanship in that regard," Lear continued, handing out what he imagined was money. "That man wields his bow as clumsily as a scarecrow. Draw me up like a tailor's measuring tape. Look, look, a mouse! Quiet now; this piece of toast will suffice. Here's my glove; I'll challenge a giant. Call up the troops. Oh, well shot, bird! Right on target, right on target!" He cheered, caught in his own world, then commanded, "Give the order."

Edgar, sensing the tension, softly mentioned, "Sweet marjoram."

King Lear dismissed it with a brief, "Pass."

. . .

Hearing the familiar voice, Gloucester whispered, "I know that voice."

Ha! Goneril, with a white beard!" King Lear exclaimed, mistaking Gloucester for someone else. "They flattered me like a dog, telling me I had white hairs before the black ones even appeared. They always agreed with everything I said—such mindless agreement isn't wisdom. When I commanded the rain to stop or the wind to cease, and it didn't, I realized they were deceiving me. They said I was everything; it's a lie, I am not immune to illness."

"The trick of that voice I do well remember. Isn't that the king?" Gloucester asked, hope flickering in his voice.

"Yes, every inch a king," Lear proclaimed, his tone grandiose. "When I glare, see how my subjects tremble. I pardon that man's life. What was your crime? Adultery? You shall not die for adultery! Even the wren engages in it, and the small gilded fly lusts before me. Let copulation flourish; Gloucester's illegitimate son has shown him more kindness than my daughters born in wedlock. Let chaos reign—I need soldiers. Look at that coy lady, her face so cold and virtuous, pretending disgust at the mention of pleasure. No creature indulges with more abandon than they do from the waist down. Women may appear human above the waist, but below, the gods give way to demons. Below there is hell, darkness, the sulfurous pit, burning, scalding, stench, decay. Oh, fie, fie, fie! Pah, pah! Fetch me some civet, good apothecary, to sweeten my thoughts. Here's your payment."

Moved by Lear's presence and ravings, Gloucester pleaded, "Oh, let me kiss that hand!"

King Lear, aware of his own disheveled state, replied, "Let me wipe it first; it smells of mortality."

Gloucester, struck by the tragic figure before him, lamented, "Oh, ruined piece of nature! This vast world will eventually wear away to nothing. Do you recognize me?"

"I remember your eyes well enough," Lear retorted, a sharp edge to his voice. "Are you squinting at me?

No, do your worst, blind Cupid! I won't love. Here, read this challenge; just note how it's written."

"Even if all the letters were as bright as suns, I couldn't see one," Gloucester confessed, his blindness absolute.

"I couldn't believe this just from hearing about it; it's true, and it breaks my heart," Edgar interjected, his voice heavy with sorrow.

"Read," commanded Lear again, oblivious to Gloucester's plight.

"With what? I have no eyes to see," Gloucester replied, his voice tinged with sadness.

"Oh, are you playing that game with me? No eyes in your head, and no money in your purse? Your eyes may be in a heavy case, but your purse is light; yet you understand how this world operates," Lear mocked.

. . .

"I understand it by feeling," Gloucester said, his tone solemn.

"What, are you mad? A man can understand how the world works without eyes. Listen with your ears: hear how that judge scolds the petty thief. Listen closely: if they switched places, who would be the judge and who the thief? Have you ever seen a farmer's dog bark at a beggar?" Lear asked, his voice rising with intensity.

"Yes, sir," Gloucester responded.

"And the beggar runs from the dog? There you might see the great image of authority: a dog obeyed because of its position," Lear declared, his tone mocking. "You scoundrel officer, hold your bloody hand! Why do you whip that prostitute? Strip your own back; you ardently desire to use her in the same way you punish her. The loan shark hangs the swindler. Small misdeeds show through tattered clothes, but robes and fur gowns hide everything. Coat sin with gold, and the strong spear of justice is rendered harmless; arm it with rags, and a dwarf's straw can pierce it. No one is guilty, I say no one; I'll vouch for them: take that from me, my friend, who has the power to silence the accusers. Get yourself glass eyes, and like a corrupt politician, pretend to see the things you do not. Now, now, now, now: pull off my boots: harder, harder: like that."

Edgar watched the unfolding scene with a blend of amazement and sorrow. "Oh, what a mix of nonsense and insight! There's reason in his madness!"

King Lear, addressing Gloucester though mistaking his identity, said, "If you want to weep for my fortunes, use my eyes. I recognize you; your name is Gloucester. You must be patient; we all come into this world crying: you know, the first time we breathe, we wail. Listen, I will preach to you; pay attention."

Gloucester, overwhelmed by the scene, could only lament, "Alack, alack the day!"

"When we are born, we cry that we have arrived on this great stage of fools," Lear continued, his voice rising with emotion. "It would be a clever trick to silence a troop of horse with soft shoes. I'll test that idea; and once I've crept up on my deceitful sons-in-law, then it will be time to strike: kill, kill, kill!"

At that moment, a gentleman entered with attendants, spotting the king. "Oh, here he is: seize him. Sir, your most dear daughter—"

"No rescue? What, am I a prisoner? I am merely fortune's fool. Treat me well, and you'll have your ransom. Get me surgeons; I feel as if my brain is injured," Lear declared, his mind clearly tormented.

"You can have anything you need," the gentleman assured him.

"No help? All alone?" Lear rambled on. "This would turn a man into salt, using his tears to water the garden and lay the dust of autumn."

"Good sir," the gentleman tried to intervene.

. . .

"I will die bravely, like a bridegroom," Lear proclaimed with a sudden shift to bravado. "What! I will be jovial: come, come; I am a king, my masters, remember that."

"You are indeed royal, and we follow your commands," the gentleman responded, affirming Lear's status.

"Then there's life in it. If you want it, you must chase me for it!" Lear exclaimed, then abruptly ran off, with the attendants quickly following him.

The gentleman, left behind, reflected on the tragic sight. "Such a pitiful sight, even for the lowliest person, is beyond words when seen in a king! You have one daughter who seems to redeem nature from the curse brought by the other two."

Edgar greeted the newcomer politely, "Hail, gentle sir."

. . .

The gentleman responded promptly, "Sir, what do you need?"

"Do you know if there's a battle coming?" Edgar asked, concern marking his tone.

"Absolutely, it's common knowledge; anyone who can hear knows that," the gentleman replied.

"But could you tell me how near the opposing army is?" Edgar pressed, seeking more specific information.

"They're close and approaching fast; the main force is expected any moment now," the gentleman explained.

"Thank you, that's all I needed to know," Edgar said, nodding his appreciation.

. . .

"Though the queen is here for a specific reason, her army has already moved forward," the gentleman added, then excused himself and left.

Left alone with Gloucester, Edgar heard the old man's plea to the heavens, "You ever-gentle gods, take my life from me; let not my darker impulses tempt me to die before it is your will!"

"Pray well, father," Edgar encouraged, showing concern.

"Now, good sir, who are you?" Gloucester asked, turning towards Edgar's voice.

"A very poor man, subdued by fortune's harsh blows; but through my own sorrows, I've developed a deep compassion. Give me your hand, I'll lead you to a safe place," Edgar offered, reaching out to the blind man.

. . .

Gloucester gratefully accepted the offer, "Hearty thanks. May the blessings of heaven continue to aid us!"

Just then, Oswald appeared, his tone triumphant and malicious. "A declared prize! Most fortunate! That blind head of yours was born to boost my fortunes. You old, unhappy traitor, remember your fate briefly: the sword meant to end your life is already drawn."

As Gloucester felt the threat of danger, he urged, "Now, let your friendly hand lend enough strength."

Edgar quickly stepped between Gloucester and Oswald, protecting the old man.

Oswald, furious, demanded, "Why do you, bold peasant, support a known traitor? Get away from him; lest his misfortune spreads to you. Let go of his arm."

. . .

Edgar stood his ground firmly. "I will not let go, sir, without further cause."

"Let go, slave, or you die!" Oswald threatened, his voice filled with menace.

"Good gentleman, go your way and let poor folks pass. If I had been scared out of my life, it wouldn't have lasted as long as it has by a fortnight. Don't come near the old man; stay back, I warn you, or I'll test whether your head or my stick is harder. I'm being honest with you," Edgar declared defiantly.

"Out, dunghill!" Oswald yelled, his insult sharp as he advanced.

"I'll knock your teeth out, sir. Come on; your thrusts don't scare me," Edgar challenged.

The confrontation escalated into a fight, and Edgar quickly overpowered Oswald, knocking him to the ground.

. . .

Gravely wounded, Oswald gasped, "Slave, you have killed me: villain, take my purse. If you ever want to prosper, bury my body; and deliver the letters you find on me to Edmund, the Earl of Gloucester; find him with the British forces. Oh, untimely death!" With those last words, Oswald died.

Edgar looked down at the fallen man. "I knew you well: a serviceable villain, as devoted to the sins of your mistress as wickedness itself would wish."

Gloucester, sensing the silence that followed the scuffle, asked, "What, is he dead?"

Edgar helped Gloucester to sit down, suggesting a moment of rest. "Let's see what's in these pockets: the letters he mentioned might help us," Edgar reasoned, acknowledging the man's death with a hint of regret that he had not met a different end. "Let's take a look. Forgive the breach of privacy, gentle wax seal, and do not judge our manners harshly. To understand our enemies, we might have to delve into their hearts; reading their papers is surely more permissible."

. . .

As he read the contents aloud, the treachery became clear:

"Let our mutual promises be remembered. You have many chances to eliminate him: if you're willing, the right time and place will soon present themselves. Nothing is settled if he returns victorious: then I am his prisoner, trapped in a marriage I despise. Save me from this detestable union, and take my place beside him.
 Your—wife, so I would say—
 Affectionate servant,
 GONERIL."

Edgar was appalled by the blatant scheming. "Oh, the boundless caprice of a woman's will! A conspiracy against a faithful husband, and to think my own brother is the replacement! Here, in the sand, I'll bury you, unsacred post of murderous desires." Edgar planned to use the incriminating letter at the right moment to expose the duke involved in this deadly plot. "It's fortunate I can relate the details of your death and this wicked business."

. . .

Gloucester, overwhelmed by the unfolding events and his own predicament, lamented his inability to escape his mental torment. "The king is mad, and how poor is my sense that I remain standing, acutely aware of my vast sorrows! It might be better if I were mad as well; then my thoughts could be detached from my pains, and my woes might lose their grip on me through misguided fantasies."

"Give me your hand," Edgar offered, sensing his father's deepening despair. As the distant sound of drums reached them, he noted, "Far off, I think I hear the drums of battle. Come, father, I'll take you to a friend." Together, they exited, moving towards an uncertain future but united by a bond of trust and mutual support.

SCENE 7

In a tent where soft music played, Lear slept on a bed, attended by his loyal followers. Cordelia, Kent, and a doctor walked in.

Cordelia addressed Kent warmly, "Oh Kent, how can I possibly live up to your goodness? My life seems too short to ever match it."

Kent responded humbly, "Madam, being recognized for my service is more than enough for me. My reports are honest, nothing more or less."

. . .

Cordelia, noticing Kent's attire, suggested, "You should change out of those clothes. They remind us of darker times. Please, take them off."

Kent, with respect, replied, "Please forgive me, madam. Remaining unknown is part of my plan. It's my request that you don't recognize me until the right time."

"Let it be as you wish, my lord," Cordelia agreed, then turned to the doctor, "How is the king doing?"

The doctor answered, "Madam, he is still sleeping."

Cordelia prayed silently, "Oh kind gods, heal the deep wounds in his troubled mind. Restore his disjointed and clashing senses, for the sake of this father changed by his trials."

The doctor suggested, "With your permission, we should wake him. He has been asleep for quite some time."

. . .

"Use your best judgment and act as you see fit," Cordelia instructed. "Is he dressed?"

"Yes, madam. In his deep sleep, we changed his clothes to fresh ones," a gentleman attending Lear confirmed.

"Be present when we wake him," the doctor advised Cordelia. "I'm confident he'll be calm."

Cordelia nodded her approval, and the doctor asked for the music to be played louder as they approached the sleeping king. "Draw closer and increase the volume of the music," he instructed.

Cordelia leaned over her father, her emotions heavy. "Oh, my dear father, let my kiss be the cure for the suffering my sisters have caused you," she whispered, pressing her lips to his forehead.

Kent looked on, moved by the scene, "Kind and dear princess!"

. . .

Cordelia continued, her voice filled with sorrow, "If you were not their father, even strangers would have felt pity at your white hair and this face, exposed to storms and thunder, and lightning. How could you, so frail, endure such hardships? Even an enemy's dog would have deserved better than you did that stormy night. And you, my poor father, had to find shelter with animals and outcasts in damp, musty straw. It's a miracle you survived with your mind intact." She paused as Lear began to stir. "He's waking up. Talk to him."

The doctor suggested, "Madam, you should speak to him. It's most appropriate."

Cordelia gently asked, "How do you feel, my royal lord? How fares your majesty?"

Lear, confused and groggy, replied, "You do me wrong to bring me back from the grave. You must be a blessed soul, while I am tormented on a wheel of fire, my own tears burning me like molten lead."

. . .

Cordelia, concerned, asked, "Sir, do you recognize me?"

"You're a spirit, aren't you? When did you die?" Lear questioned, still delirious.

Cordelia sighed, realizing the depth of his confusion. "He's not fully awake yet. Give him some time," the doctor advised.

Lear, struggling with his reality, murmured, "Where have I been? Where am I? Is this daylight? I am deeply hurt. I'd pity anyone else feeling like this. I'm not even sure these hands are mine. Let me see; I can feel this pinprick. I wish I could be sure of my own state."

Cordelia gently urged Lear to look at her, "Please, look at me, sir, and bless me with your hands. No, sir, you must not kneel."

Lear, bewildered and frail, pleaded, "Please, don't tease me. I'm just a foolish old man, well past eighty years. I must admit, I don't think I'm fully sane. I feel like I should recognize you and this man here, but I'm not sure. I don't know where I am, and these clothes are unfamiliar to me. I don't remember where I slept last night. Please, don't laugh at me. I believe this lady to be my daughter Cordelia."

Cordelia confirmed softly, "And so I am."

Lear, tears forming in his eyes, said, "Are your tears real? Please, don't cry. If you have poison for me, I'll drink it. I remember now, your sisters did harm me, and you had reasons to dislike me, though they did not."

Cordelia reassured him tenderly, "No cause, no cause."

Lear, still confused, asked, "Am I in France?"

Kent corrected him, "No, sir, you're in your own kingdom."

. . .

Lear, cautious, replied, "Please, don't deceive me."

The doctor, observing Lear's fragile state, advised Cordelia, "He's calmer now, but it's risky to make him recall what he's lost. Suggest he go inside and don't disturb him further until he's more settled."

Cordelia invited Lear gently, "Would it please your highness to walk?"

Lear requested, "Please be patient with me. Forget and forgive; I am old and foolish."

After they exited, a gentleman inquired of Kent, "Is it true that the Duke of Cornwall was killed?"

Kent confirmed, "Yes, it's certain."

The gentleman asked about who led Cornwall's forces now, to which Kent replied, "It's said to be the illegitimate son of Gloucester."

. . .

"The banished son Edgar is rumored to be with the Earl of Kent in Germany," the gentleman added.

Kent noted, "Things are uncertain. It's time to be vigilant; the kingdom's forces are nearing."

The gentleman predicted, "The coming conflict is likely to be violent. Farewell, sir."

With the gentleman gone, Kent resolved, "My actions will have their full effect, for better or worse, depending on how today's battle goes." He then left to prepare.

ACT V

SCENE 1

In the British camp near Dover, Edmund, Regan, and their soldiers made their entrance with the sound of drums and the display of colors. Edmund spoke to one of his men, urging him to find out if the duke still planned to proceed as intended, or if recent advice had led him to reconsider. He noted the duke was known for changing his mind and often second-guessed himself.

Regan, looking concerned, turned to Edmund and said, "It seems likely that something unfortunate has happened to our sister's man."

"I'm afraid that might be true," Edmund replied.

. . .

"Now, my sweet lord," Regan continued, her voice softening, "you know how well I wish you. Tell me the truth—do you love my sister?"

Edmund responded with respect, "Yes, I hold her in high honor."

"But have you ever sought out my brother in secret?" Regan pressed, suspicion tinting her voice.

"You are mistaken," Edmund assured her firmly.

Regan's tone hardened as she confessed her feelings, "I can't stand her, my lord. Please, keep your distance from her."

"Don't worry about me," Edmund replied calmly, trying to assuage her fears, "It's she and her husband, the duke, who should concern us."

. . .

Just then, Albany, Goneril, and more soldiers arrived with similar fanfare. Goneril muttered to herself, preferring to lose the battle than see her sister win Edmund's affection.

Albany greeted them warmly, "It's good to see you, sister." Then he shared news that the king had joined his daughter, forced into action by the harsh demands of their rule. He confessed, "I've never been brave where I couldn't be honest. This war touches us all closely, as France is invading our land, and I'm afraid many have just cause to oppose us."

Edmund nodded in agreement with Albany's words, "Sir, you speak with honor."

Regan, looking puzzled, asked, "Why are we discussing this now?"

Goneril interjected, her voice firm, "Let's unite against our common enemy. These personal squabbles shouldn't distract us here."

. . .

Albany proposed a plan, "Let's consult with the experienced warriors about our strategy."

"I'll join you shortly at your tent," Edmund replied, ready to follow Albany's lead.

Turning to her sister, Regan asked, "Are you coming with us, sister?"

Goneril responded flatly, "No."

"It would be wise for you to come," Regan insisted.

Goneril, musing to herself about understanding the underlying issues, relented, "Fine, I'll join you."

As they prepared to leave, Edgar, disguised and unrecognizable, approached them. He caught Albany's attention, "If you've ever given time to someone as lowly as me, please hear me out."

. . .

"I'll catch up with you," Albany told the others, signaling them to go ahead, leaving him with Edgar.

Once they were alone, Edgar handed Albany a letter, "Please read this before the battle. If we win, have the trumpets honor the messenger. Though I appear downtrodden, I have a champion who can validate the claims in this letter. If we lose, then all our worldly designs come to an end, and all schemes stop. I wish you good fortune."

Albany, intrigued, asked Edgar to stay while he read the letter. "Stay till I have read the letter."

"I was told not to wait," Edgar responded. "When the time is right, just signal, and I'll come back."

"Very well, I'll look over your letter then," Albany concluded as Edgar left the scene.

Edmund re-entered, urgency in his voice. "The enemy is in sight; gather your forces. I've estimated their strength and numbers through careful scouting, but we must act quickly."

Albany acknowledged the need for haste, "We will seize the moment." With that, he departed.

Left alone, Edmund contemplated his tangled relationships with Goneril and Regan. "I've pledged my love to both sisters, each as suspicious of the other as one bitten by a snake. Which should I choose? Both? One? Or none? If both live, neither can be truly mine. Choosing the widow will only enrage Goneril, and with her husband still alive, my position remains precarious. We'll use his leadership for now in the battle, and afterwards, let those who wish him gone plot his removal. As for any mercy Albany plans for Lear and Cordelia, once the battle is over and they are captured, they will not be pardoned. My duty is to defend, not to discuss." With his plans set, Edmund exited to prepare for the looming conflict.

SCENE 2

In the clamor of the battlefield, King Lear and his daughter Cordelia marched across with their soldiers, colors flying and drums beating, before disappearing from sight. Shortly after, Edgar and Gloucester entered the scene.

Edgar gestured to a nearby tree, offering its shade to Gloucester. "Here, father, rest under this tree for now. Pray for our success. If I come back, I'll bring you good news."

"May grace follow you," Gloucester replied, his voice filled with a weary hope.

. . .

After Edgar left, the sounds of battle shifted, signaling a retreat. Edgar quickly reappeared, urgency etched on his face. "Hurry, old man, take my hand and let's go! King Lear and Cordelia have been captured."

Gloucester, exhausted and resigned, replied, "No more, I can go no further; one might as well perish right here."

Edgar, trying to lift his father's spirits, encouraged him. "Why fall back into despair? We must accept our fates as they come, as we accepted our lives at birth. Being ready is all that matters; come on."

Gloucester conceded with a nod, acknowledging the truth in Edgar's words, "And that's true too."

Together, they left the field, the echoes of battle fading behind them.

SCENE 3

In the chaotic aftermath of battle, Edmund, with an air of authority, instructed some officers to take King Lear and Cordelia into custody. "Keep them safe until we decide their fate," he commanded.

Cordelia, bound by chains yet resilient in spirit, turned to her father, the deposed king. "We aren't the first to suffer despite our good intentions. I am brought low for your sake, Father, and would stand strong against misfortune if not for you."

King Lear, his face lined with sorrow and madness, rejected the thought of seeing his other daughters.

"No, let's not. Let's go to the prison," he insisted, his voice brittle. "There, just the two of us can live like birds trapped in a cage. When you seek my blessing, I'll ask for your forgiveness instead. We'll live out our days praying, singing, and laughing at trivial matters, discussing news from the court as if we were mere observers, understanding the universe as though we were divine spies. We'll outlast the influential, who rise and fall with the changing tides."

Edmund's voice snapped them back to reality. "Take them away now," he ordered sharply.

As they were led away, Lear spoke to Cordelia with a tone mixed with resolve and despair. "On such sacrifices, my dear Cordelia, the gods look favorably. If we are parted, it shall be by divine intervention, not human hands. Dry your tears; grief shall not consume us before we see them suffer. Let's go."

Once the king and his daughter had departed under guard, Edmund turned to a captain nearby, handing him a note. "Follow them to prison," he whispered, sliding the paper into the man's hand. "This promotion is just the beginning for you. Follow these instructions, and you'll climb to high ranks. Remember, we must be as ruthless as the times demand. Don't question your orders—either commit to them or find another way to succeed."

The captain nodded at Edmund's instructions, his resolve clear. "I'll handle it, my lord."

"Proceed immediately, and let me know once it's done. Follow the plan exactly as I've outlined," Edmund replied firmly.

With a hint of dry humor, the captain quipped, "I'm no horse to pull a cart or eat oats, but if it's a man's job, consider it done." He then left to carry out his orders.

Soon after, Albany, along with Goneril, Regan, another captain, and soldiers, made their entrance. The air was tense with the aftermath of conflict.

Albany, addressing Edmund with a formal nod, commended him. "You've demonstrated great bravery today, and fortune has favored you with valuable prisoners from the opposing side. We expect you to manage them judiciously, based on their actions and our security needs."

Edmund responded with a calculated tone. "I found it prudent to place the old and despairing King Lear under secure watch. His venerable age and his title might sway public sentiment in his favor, threatening to turn our own forces against us. Alongside him, I've detained the queen, Queen Cordelia. They will be available to stand trial at your convenience, whether tomorrow or later. We are all exhausted and have lost much today. The matter of Cordelia and her father should be discussed in a more appropriate setting."

Albany's patience seemed to thin as he interjected, "I must remind you, sir, that in this conflict, you remain a subject, not an equal."

Regan quickly added, siding with Edmund but with a sharp tone, "We may choose to elevate him as we see fit. He led our forces and acted on my authority; he deserves recognition as your equal."

. . .

Goneril intervened, her voice cutting through the tension. "Let's not overstate his role. He's elevating himself more by his own merit than by what we've conferred upon him."

Regan, asserting her authority, confidently stated, "In my right, which invests him, he stands shoulder to shoulder with the best."

Goneril, not missing a beat, retorted, "That would indeed be the highest honor, if you were to marry him."

"Often, jesters turn out to be prophets," Regan shot back, her words tinged with a foreboding wisdom.

Goneril, unimpressed, responded sharply, "Be careful! The eyes that see that future are squinting."

Regan, feeling the strain of the situation, admitted, "I am unwell, or I would respond more sharply.

General, take my soldiers, my prisoners, my inheritance. Command them and even command me—the control is yours. Let the world see that I appoint you here as my lord and master."

Goneril, incredulous, asked, "Do you actually plan to enjoy his company as your lord?"

Albany interjected firmly, "That decision is not yours to make."

Edmund, facing Albany, declared boldly, "Nor is it yours, lord."

Albany, his patience waning, snapped back, "Yes, it is, you who are of mixed loyalty."

Regan, turning to Edmund, called for action, "Let the drums beat to affirm my claim on you."

Albany, however, was not finished. "Hold on; listen to reason. Edmund, I arrest you for high treason." He then pointed accusingly at Goneril, "And you, disguised as loyalty, are nothing but treachery."

Addressing Goneril, Albany continued, "Your claim is void as it concerns my wife, who is promised to this man. And as her husband, I oppose this union. Should you wish to marry, address your affections to me, for my wife is already promised."

Goneril scoffed at the unfolding drama, "What an interlude this is!"

Albany, resolute and armored for conflict, threw down his glove, a challenge to Edmund. "If no one can prove your treason, then I will. Let the trumpet sound. I will prove upon your heart, before I even eat, that you are exactly as guilty as I have declared."

Regan, pale and unsteady, moaned, "Sick, oh, so very sick!"

. . .

Goneril muttered to herself, wary of the unfolding scene, "If this doesn't end as I expect, I'll never trust my schemes again."

Edmund, defiant and enraged, threw down his glove in challenge. "Here's my answer. Whoever calls me a traitor is lying through his teeth. Sound the trumpet! Let anyone who dares, come forward. I stand firm in my truth and honor."

Albany, seizing control of the situation, called for a herald. "A herald, ho!"

Echoing him, Edmund shouted, "A herald, ho, indeed!"

Albany, turning to Edmund with a cold smile, said, "Trust only in your own courage; your soldiers, raised in my name, have been discharged under my command."

As the tension escalated, Regan's condition worsened. "My illness intensifies," she gasped.

Albany quickly ordered her to be taken to his tent for care. As she was led away, a herald arrived at Albany's command.

"Come here, herald. Let the trumpet sound and proclaim the challenge," Albany instructed.

The captain commanded, "Sound, trumpet!" and the trumpet blared.

The herald then read the proclamation: "'If any man of rank or station in the army believes Edmund, supposed Earl of Gloucester, to be a traitor, let him come forth at the third trumpet call. Edmund stands ready to defend his honor.'"

Edmund, filled with a mix of defiance and anticipation, commanded, "Sound!"

The herald obeyed, the first trumpet call echoing through the camp.

. . .

"Again!" Edmund insisted.

The second trumpet sounded.

"Once more!" demanded Edmund.

After the third trumpet call, a figure appeared in response—an armed Edgar, with a trumpet heralding his entrance.

Albany, curious and cautious, addressed the newcomer. "Ask him his intentions, why he answers this call of the trumpet."

The herald, following procedure, asked, "Who are you? State your name and rank, and explain why you have answered this summons."

Edgar responded, his voice steady but his identity hidden, "My name has been erased, eaten away by treason's destructive force. Yet, I remain as noble as the man I face today."

Albany, intrigued, inquired, "And who is this adversary?"

"Who here represents Edmund, Earl of Gloucester?" Edgar asked, scanning the crowd.

Edmund stepped forward, declaring, "I am he. What do you have to say to me?"

Edgar was resolute, his voice ringing clear. "Draw your sword. If my words offend a noble heart, let your sword bring justice. Here is mine," he said, presenting his sword. "I stand by my honor, my oath, and my duty. Despite your youth, your recent victories, and your high rank, you are a traitor. You've betrayed your gods, your brother, and your father; you've conspired against this distinguished prince. From the top of your head to the soles of your feet, you are utterly corrupt. If you deny this, I am ready to prove it with my sword against your heart."

. . .

Edmund, his pride wounded, retorted, "Normally, I would ask for your name, but your appearance and eloquent speech suggest nobility, which I won't question now. I throw back these accusations of treason at you. Your lies barely scratch the surface, but my sword will drive them home, to rest there forever. Let the trumpets sound!"

As the trumpets blared, they engaged in combat. Amidst the clashing of their swords, Edmund was struck down.

Albany, seeing Edmund fall, urgently called out, "Save him, save him!"

Goneril, watching the scene unfold, remarked coldly, "This is merely a scheme, Gloucester. According to the laws of combat, you weren't obligated to accept a challenge from someone unknown. You haven't been defeated in true combat but tricked and misled."

Albany, enraged by Goneril's defiance, brandished a letter threateningly. "Silence, woman, or I'll use this paper to stop your words," he snapped, holding the letter out to Edmund. "You, more vile than any name could express, read of your own misdeeds." He forced the letter into Edmund's hands, and Goneril, realizing the gravity of her situation, chose to exit hastily rather than face further questioning.

"Follow her; she's desperate and dangerous," Albany commanded, his attention quickly returning to Edmund.

Edmund, fatally wounded, confessed openly, "What you've accused me of, I have indeed committed, and even more. Time would have revealed it all, but my time is up. Yet, who are you, who have brought my downfall? If you are noble, I forgive you."

Edgar, his presence solemn and his tone forgiving, responded, "Let us forgive each other. I am no less noble than you, Edmund. In fact, perhaps more so because of the wrongs you've done me. I am Edgar, your brother, the son of the father you betrayed. The gods often use our own sins as the means to punish us. The dark deeds that gave you life cost our father his sight."

. . .

Edmund acknowledged the justice in Edgar's words. "You speak the truth; everything has come full circle. I am here, at the end."

Albany, moved by the revelation and Edgar's nobility, exclaimed, "I sensed a royal dignity in you. My heart would break if I ever bore any hatred towards you or your father."

"I know you held no ill will, noble prince," Edgar replied, acknowledging Albany's sentiment.

Albany, curious about Edgar's journey, asked, "Where have you been hiding? How did you endure seeing your father suffer?"

Edgar began to recount his harrowing tale, his voice heavy with emotion. "I disguised myself to escape the death sentence that followed me so closely. I adopted the rags of a madman, an appearance so lowly that even dogs looked down on me. In this guise, I encountered my father after he had been blinded, his eyes gouged out and the rings around them bleeding. I guided him, begged for him, and saved him from utter despair. Yet, I never revealed my identity to him until just a short while ago when I was armed and hopeful of success. I asked for his blessing and finally told him the full story of my struggles. But the joy and grief of it were too much for his weakened heart, and it burst with a mixture of both emotions, ending his life with a final, joyful smile."

Edmund, visibly moved by Edgar's account, acknowledged, "Your words have touched me deeply, and might yet bring some good. Continue, though it looks like you have more to share."

Albany, overwhelmed by the tale of suffering, pleaded, "If there is more, and it is even more sorrowful, please hold it back; I feel ready to break down just hearing all this."

Edgar, sensing the burden of his words, replied, "What I've told you might seem like an ending for those who shy away from sorrow, but there's more that could further deepen our grief." He continued,

"While I was loudly lamenting my state, a man who once avoided me due to my miserable condition, recognized me. He embraced me tightly, overwhelmed with emotion, and cried out as if he would burst the heavens. He then threw himself on my father, sharing a heart-wrenching story of King Lear and his own trials that was so moving, his sorrow intensified and it seemed like his life might just snap under the strain. I had to leave him in that overwhelmed state after the trumpets called twice."

Albany, curious, inquired, "But who was this man?"

"It was Kent," Edgar revealed. "The same Kent who was banished. He disguised himself and followed his king, serving him in ways that no servant should have to."

Just then, a gentleman entered hurriedly, a bloody knife in hand, crying out for help.

Edgar, immediately on alert, asked, "What help do you need?"

. . .

Albany urged the man to explain, "Speak, man. What does that bloody knife mean?"

The gentleman, breathless and shocked, managed to say, "It's still hot—it came straight from the heart of —oh, she's dead!"

Albany demanded urgently, "Who is dead? Speak, man."

"Your lady, sir, your lady: and her sister has been poisoned; she confessed it herself," the gentleman disclosed, the gravity of the news hitting everyone present.

Edmund, realizing the full extent of the tragedy, remarked bitterly, "I was betrothed to both sisters; now, all three of us are united in death."

As they processed this grim news, Edgar noted, "Here comes Kent."

. . .

As the grim scene unfolded, Albany, shaken yet resolute, commanded, "Bring their bodies here, whether they are alive or dead. This divine judgment that makes us tremble is beyond our pity." With a wave of his hand, he sent the gentleman off to carry out his orders.

Kent then entered, his presence bringing a solemn air with him. Albany, recognizing him but pressed for time, remarked, "Oh, is this he? There's no time for the courtesies that propriety demands."

Kent, filled with a mournful purpose, responded, "I have come to say goodnight to my king and master. Isn't he here?"

Albany, reminded of the grave matters at hand, urgently asked Edmund, "Where is the king? And where's Cordelia? Kent, do you see this dreadful sight?" The bodies of Goneril and Regan were then brought in, stark reminders of the tragedy that had unfolded.

. . .

Kent, gazing upon the scene, lamented, "Alas, why has it come to this?"

Edmund, acknowledging the chaos caused by his schemes, confessed, "Yet I was loved. One sister poisoned the other for my sake, and then she killed herself."

"Indeed, cover their faces," Albany instructed somberly, unable to bear the sight of the fallen sisters.

Despite his injuries, a sense of urgency surged through Edmund. "I'm fighting for my life but there's some good I still hope to do, against my own nature. Send someone quickly to the castle; my orders concerning the lives of Lear and Cordelia might still be carried out—hurry, send help in time!"

"Run, run, oh, run!" Albany cried out, desperate to prevent further tragedy.

. . .

Edgar, quick to respond, asked, "To whom, my lord? Who holds the power to stop this? Give them a sign of reprieve."

Edmund, grasping at redemption, instructed, "Good thinking—take my sword, give it to the captain as my token."

Albany, recognizing the urgency, echoed, "Haste thee, as if your life depends on it."

As Edgar hurried off, Edmund revealed the grim reality, "He has orders from your wife and me to hang Cordelia in the prison, and to make it seem as though she killed herself in despair." The truth of his previous machinations now laid bare in his final moments.

Edmund was carried off by the soldiers at Albany's command, his fate uncertain but grim. The air was heavy with tension and sorrow, a silence that was abruptly shattered by the tragic re-entry of King Lear, cradling the lifeless body of his daughter

Cordelia in his arms. Edgar, the captain, and others followed solemnly behind.

Lear's grief was palpable as he cried out to the heavens, "Howl, howl, howl, howl! Oh, you might as well be made of stone. If I had your tongues and eyes, I'd scream and cry so loudly that the heavens themselves would crack. She's gone forever! I can tell the difference between life and death; she's as dead as the dirt. Bring me a mirror; if her breath fogs it up, then she must still be alive."

Kent, witnessing the heartbreaking scene, questioned despairingly, "Is this the promised end?"

Kent, standing steadfast beside his king, noted the irony of fate: "If fortune brags of loving and hating, we see one of her favorites fallen here."

Lear, weary and confused, looked at Kent, squinting, "This is a dull sight. Are you Kent?"

. . .

Kent confirmed, "The same, your servant Kent. And where do you think your servant Caius is?"

Lear, with a fleeting touch of his former sharpness, replied, "He's a good man, strong and quick to act. But he's dead and gone."

"No, my good lord; I am that very man," Kent revealed, showing that he was indeed Caius in disguise.

Lear, struggling to comprehend, insisted, "I'll see that for myself."

Kent, with loyalty unyielded by the years of disguise and hardship, explained, "I have followed your troubled steps from the start of your decline."

"You are welcome here," Lear responded, a glimmer of recognition in his tone.

. . .

Kent's outlook remained grim, "And no one else is. Everything is cheerless, dark, and deadly. Your eldest daughters have destroyed themselves, and are indeed dead."

Lear, his mind shadowed by grief, murmured in agreement, "Ay, so I think."

Albany, observing Lear's deteriorating state, commented, "He knows not what he says, and it's futile to try to make him understand our presence here."

Edgar agreed, "It's truly pointless."

At that moment, a captain entered with news, "Edmund is dead, my lord."

Albany, surrounded by the gravity of so many tragedies, dismissed the news as minor, "That's but a trifle here."

. . .

Addressing those gathered, he declared, "You lords and noble friends, understand our intentions. Any comfort we can offer in this time of decay will be given. For the remainder of this old king's life, I will cede my power to him." Turning to Edgar and Kent, he continued, "And you, to your rightful status, along with rewards fitting the honor you've more than earned. All friends shall reap the rewards of their virtue, and all foes will suffer as they deserve. Oh, see, see!"

Edgar, equally horrified, added, "Or an image of that horror?"

Albany, overwhelmed by the unfolding disaster, could only utter, "Fall, and cease!"

Lear, desperate for any sign of life, noticed a feather stir and clung to hope. "She lives! If it's true, it's a miracle that redeems all the sorrows I've ever felt."

Kent, moved by his master's plight, knelt beside him, exclaiming, "Oh, my good master!"

. . .

Lear, blinded by grief and unable to recognize him, dismissed him, "Prithee, away."

Edgar intervened, reminding Lear, "It's noble Kent, your friend."

But Lear, consumed by rage and despair, lashed out, "A plague upon you, murderers, traitors all! I might have saved her; now she's gone forever! Cordelia, Cordelia, stay just a moment. Ha! What do you say? Her voice was always soft, gentle, and low—an excellent thing in a woman. I killed the slave that was hanging you."

The captain confirmed Lear's claim, "It's true, my lords, he did."

Lear, turning to the captain, asked, "Did I not, fellow? In my prime, with my good sharp sword, I would have made them skip. I am old now, and these troubles weigh me down. Who are you? My eyes aren't what they used to be; I'll tell you straight."

. . .

Kent, standing steadfast beside his king, noted the irony of fate: "If fortune brags of loving and hating, we see one of her favorites fallen here."

Lear, weary and confused, looked at Kent, squinting, "This is a dull sight. Are you Kent?"

Kent confirmed, "The same, your servant Kent. And where do you think your servant Caius is?"

Lear, with a fleeting touch of his former sharpness, replied, "He's a good man, strong and quick to act. But he's dead and gone."

"No, my good lord; I am that very man," Kent revealed, showing that he was indeed Caius in disguise.

Lear, struggling to comprehend, insisted, "I'll see that for myself."

. . .

Kent, with loyalty unyielded by the years of disguise and hardship, explained, "I have followed your troubled steps from the start of your decline."

"You are welcome here," Lear responded, a glimmer of recognition in his tone.

Kent's outlook remained grim, "And no one else is. Everything is cheerless, dark, and deadly. Your eldest daughters have destroyed themselves, and are indeed dead."

Lear, his mind shadowed by grief, murmured in agreement, "Ay, so I think."

Albany, observing Lear's deteriorating state, commented, "He knows not what he says, and it's futile to try to make him understand our presence here."

Edgar agreed, "It's truly pointless."

. . .

At that moment, a captain entered with news, "Edmund is dead, my lord."

Albany, surrounded by the gravity of so many tragedies, dismissed the news as minor, "That's but a trifle here."

Addressing those gathered, he declared, "You lords and noble friends, understand our intentions. Any comfort we can offer in this time of decay will be given. For the remainder of this old king's life, I will cede my power to him." Turning to Edgar and Kent, he continued, "And you, to your rightful status, along with rewards fitting the honor you've more than earned. All friends shall reap the rewards of their virtue, and all foes will suffer as they deserve. Oh, see, see!"

As King Lear held Cordelia in his arms, his grief turned into despair, "And my poor fool is hanged! No, no, no life! Why should a dog, a horse, a rat, have life, and you have none at all? You'll never come again. Never, never, never, never, never!" Overcome by sorrow, he requested, "Pray you, undo this button: thank you, sir. Do you see this? Look at her, look, her lips, look there, look there!" With those final words, he drew his last breath and died.

Edgar, startled and distressed, cried out, "He faints! My lord, my lord!"

Kent, his heart breaking, pleaded softly, "Break, heart; I pray thee, break!"

Edgar urged, "Look up, my lord."

Kent, respecting the peace that death brought Lear, said solemnly, "Vex not his ghost: Oh, let him pass! He who would try to stretch his spirit on the rack of this harsh world does him great hate."

Edgar confirmed the inevitable, "He is gone, indeed."

Kent reflected on Lear's tumultuous life, "The wonder is, he endured so long: he but usurped his life."

. . .

Albany, taking charge in the wake of such overwhelming tragedy, ordered, "Bear them from hence. Our present business is general woe." Turning to Kent and Edgar, he entrusted them with leadership, "Friends of my soul, you two rule in this realm, and sustain the wounded state."

Kent, feeling the pull of his own fate, responded, "I have a journey, sir, shortly to go; my master calls me, I must not say no."

Albany, acknowledging the heavy burden they all carried, concluded, "The weight of this sad time we must obey; speak what we feel, not what we ought to say. The oldest hath borne most: we that are young shall never see so much, nor live so long."

As they exited, the somber tones of a dead march played, escorting them and marking the end of an era fraught with suffering and strife.

THE END

FURTHER READING

King Lear's Exploration of Authority and Human Suffering: Written by Shakespeare in the early 17th century, "King Lear" delves deeply into the themes of authority, justice, and the human condition. The tragic narrative reflects on the complexities of kinship and loyalty.

The Division of the Kingdom: Lear's decision to divide his kingdom among his daughters underlies the play's drama. This division is not merely political but symbolic, reflecting themes of broken trust, the vanity of power, and the frailty of human judgments.

. . .

Lear's Madness and its Symbolic Importance: As Lear descends into madness, his journey symbolizes the human struggle with self-awareness and enlightenment under duress. His madness is a central motif that exposes the vulnerability and inherent flaws of humanity.

The Storm as a Catalyst: The fierce storm in "King Lear" acts both as a physical and metaphorical upheaval. It represents nature's response to the moral chaos unleashed by Lear's abdication of responsibility and his daughters' treachery.

Themes of Vision and Blindness: The play frequently addresses metaphors of sight and blindness, particularly through the characters of Lear and Gloucester. Their physical and metaphorical blindness leads to personal revelation and tragic downfall, highlighting the theme of moral and psychological insight.

Justice and Morality: "King Lear" scrutinizes the themes of justice and morality in a world that often seems devoid of these qualities. The harsh treatment of characters like Cordelia and Kent juxtaposes the evil machinations of Goneril, Regan, and Edmund, presenting a bleak view of human nature.

The Role of the Fool: The Fool is not just a source of comic relief but a voice of truth and reason. His interactions with Lear serve as a critique of the king's decisions and provide critical commentary on events unfolding within the play.

Elements of Tragedy: "King Lear" is a profound exploration of tragedy, characterized by the high status of the protagonist, his tragic flaw, and the eventual catharsis experienced by the audience. The tragic elements underscore the themes of loss and redemption.

Family Dynamics and Betrayal: At its heart, the play is a dramatic portrayal of family and betrayal. The dynamics between Lear and his daughters, and Gloucester with his sons, reveal the destructive power of ambition and betrayal within familial relationships.

. . .

Lear's Reconciliation and Death: The play culminates in Lear's tragic recognition and reconciliation with Cordelia, only to face the ultimate tragedy of her death. This ending emphasizes the themes of redemption and the cruel unpredictability of life.

Performance History and Adaptations: Like "The Tempest," "King Lear" has a rich performance history, adapting over centuries to reflect contemporary themes and concerns. It has been staged in various forms, influencing countless adaptations in film, television, and theatre.

Legacy and Continued Relevance: "King Lear" remains a pivotal work in literature and drama, its themes of power, betrayal, and redemption resonating through the ages. Its examination of the human spirit continues to challenge and inspire audiences and readers worldwide.

ABOUT THE AUTHOR

Jeanette Vigon is a vibrant storyteller hailing from the sun-kissed beaches of California, where her Spanish heritage infuses her writing with a colorful  zest for life. Born to Spanish immigrants who carried stories of their homeland across the ocean, Jeanette's childhood was rich with tales that sparked her imagination and sowed the seeds for her future in storytelling.

After completing her education with a focus on early childhood development, Jeanette dedicated herself to the noble profession of teaching. As a beloved primary school teacher, she spent years enlightening young minds in the classroom. Her magical ability to turn even the most mundane lesson into a memorable adventure earned her admiration from both her pupils and peers.

However, the call of the pen proved too strong for Jeanette to ignore. Diving headfirst into the world of literature, she transitioned from shaping minds with chalk to enchanting them with words as a full-time writer. Her intimate knowledge of children's learning styles, combined with her rich cultural roots, enables her to craft stories that are not only engaging but also educational.

Jeanette's writing is characterized by its empathy, humor, and a deep understanding of what captivates children's hearts and minds. Whether retelling a classic Shakespearean tale or penning an original story, her books are beloved for their ability to bridge cultural gaps and bring diverse experiences to the forefront of children's literature.

Now, with several acclaimed titles to her name, Jeanette continues to share her passion for enriching young lives through reading. When she's not lost in her latest manuscript, you can find her indulging in her love for travel, exploring new destinations, and collecting fresh inspirations for her next enchanting narrative.

It's hard for books to get noticed these days. Whether you liked this one or not, please consider writing a review, thanks!

Jeanette Vigon

Printed in Great Britain
by Amazon